# Baba's Vaani

## His Sayings and Teachings

# *Sterling titles on Shirdi Sai Baba*

Baba's Rinanubandh: Leelas during His Sojourn in Shirdi
*Vinny Chitluri*

Shirdi Sai Speaks... Sab Ka Malik Ek
Quotes for the Day

Sai Hari Katha
*Dasganu Maharaj*

108 Names of Shirdi Sai Baba

SHRI SAI SATCHARITA: The Life and Teachings of Shirdi Sai Baba
*Govind R Dabholkar*

Shri Sai Baba's Teachings & Philosophy
*Lt Col M B Nimbalkar*

Sai Baba's 261 Leelas
*Balkrishna Panday*

Shirdi Sai Baba and Other Perfect Masters
*C B Satpathy*

I am always with you
*Lorraine Walshe-Ryan*

Unravelling the Enigma: Shirdi Sai Baba in the Light of Sufism (Rev. Edn.)
*Marrianne Warren*

God Who Walked on Earth: The Life & Times of Shirdi Sai Baba
*R Parthasarathy*

Shri Shirdi Sai Baba: His Life and Miracles

Life History of Shirdi Sai Baba
*Ammula Sambasiva Rao*

Sai Baba: His Divine Glimpses
*V B Kher*

Sri Sai Baba
*Sai Sharan Anand*

A Solemn Pledge from True Tales of Shirdi Sai Baba
*Dr B H Briz-Kishore*

# Baba's Vaani

## His Sayings and Teachings

*Compiled by*
**Vinny Chitluri**

**STERLING PAPERBACKS**
An imprint of
Sterling Publishers (P) Ltd.
A-59, Okhla Industrial Area, Phase-II,
New Delhi-110020.
Tel: 26387070, 26386209; Fax: 91-11-26383788
E-mail: mail@sterlingpublishers.com
ghai@nde.vsnl.net.in
www.sterlingpublishers.com

*Baba's Vaani: His Sayings and Teachings*
© 2008, Vinny Chitluri
ISBN 978 81 207 3859 1
Reprint 2011, 2012

Printed in India

*Printed and Published by* Sterling Publishers Pvt. Ltd.,
New Delhi-110 020.

# Introduction

Hari Sitaram Dixit or Kaka Sahib as Baba called him had a wonderful habit of keeping a diary. Many of the other devotees also did the same. Meticulously he wrote Baba's *leelas* as they unfolded before him. Every letter, every note that he received from the devotees he preserved. Most importantly, he wrote Baba's words and sayings. For they give a great deal of insights into Baba's moods, like sham rage which in actuality was a blessing in disguise, and Baba's teachings.

Unfortunately, unlike Ganesh Shrikrishna Khaparde he has not mentioned the dates. Nonetheless, the diary is a gem and is priceless. The *leelas* from his diary were published in the *Sai Leela Magazine* in the early 1920s. Most of the *leelas* given below are from his diary.

I for one thank Kaka Sahib, for enriching the lives of many devotees of Baba by his contribution of 'The Dixit Diary'.

Especially in the parables, Baba flits from one topic to another. The English translation is nearly impossible. Since this book is about Baba's *Vaani*, it has been translated verbatim. Therefore, it is impossible for the English translation to do justice to the 'sayings'. No translation can bring out the nuances of the original, and therefore the reader may find that the language does not flow naturally.

Baba when he spoke Marathi or Hindi it was colloquial, so it's even harder to write it in English. He used words like *arre, re* and *kayko*, just to mention a few.

This book is a kaleidoscope of Baba's *leelas*, some parables, his sayings and his *bodha paddhati*. Baba had an unique way of teaching, by way of *dakshina*, parables and even directly.

This book is Baba's, but the imperfections are definitely mine.

# Acknowledgements

Baba gave me many gifts in my life, and some of them were in the form of guardian angels. These angels helped me in many ways. Most importantly they helped me when I was writing this book. I take this opportunity to thank them from the bottom of my heart.

To Sada S Ghode, I owe a debt of gratitude for doing everything that was required to be done in this book, from searching for the descendants of Baba's *bhaktas* to learning the intricate computer.

Sandeep E Gondkar of Shirdi, an advocate by profession but a computer wizard, and god sent for me.

Neeta Shebde of Pune, for sending me photographs of the devotees residing in Pune so I did not have to make the trips to Pune.

Sri Krishna Kapur, New Delhi whose *rinanubandhic* ties with me made this book possible. He helped me in innumerable ways, they are far too many to mention.

S K Ghai of Sterling Publishers, New Delhi who treated me like a family member, and most importantly for publishing my book.

I owe a debt of gratitude to Manjula S of Bangaluru, my spiritual guru. Thank you Manjula for interpreting all these difficult Sanskrit words, and parables for me.

# Contents

*Leela 1:*     # Padmanabandra Swami from Alandi

This *leela* is given in *Shri Sai Satcharita* Chapter 13. In the *Sai Leela Magazine* of 1923, the Swami himself has written a detailed account. It is given below.

He states, "Following the advice of beloved Shriman Hari Sitaram Dixit, residing in Mumbai, I visited Shirdi." He further states, and I quote.

"By the grace of Shri Sai Baba, I am enveloped by an abundance of joy. After my pilgrimage to Shirdi, I returned on Thursday the 29th of January and proceeded to Alandi. There I attended the *punyatithi* (death anniversary) of Shri Guru Maharaj (Tukaram) on the 2nd of February. On the following day which was Tuesday I went to Mumbai.

"There I consulted Dr Underwood regarding the swelling behind my ear, extending to the neck. His advice was 'No surgery is required'. He then gave me an injection of some serum. He further added, 'This will take care of the swelling.'"

He then narrates his experience at Shirdi. "It is impossible to describe the lustrous divinity of Shri Sai Maharaj. The effect was mind boggling, and I got immense peace."

## Prarabdha karma has to be borne

"Many of the devotees gathered there advised me to tell Sai Maharaj about the swelling. But from my heart and soul I was disinclined to do so. The reason for not doing so was that I had gone solely to have his *darshan*, without any ulterior motive. I strongly believe that the *prarabdha* karma (karma or actions which have already started yielding the fruits) has to be borne by me. Ultimately I asked Madhavrao

(Shama) to tell Maharaj about my problem. Accordingly he brought up the topic while I was having *darshan*. Maharaj said lovingly, '*Allah sab accha karega*' (Allah will make everything all right.) At that very moment my troubled mind became calm.

"The doctor at Nagpur had advised surgery, so did the doctor from Alandi. They were consulted prior to my visit to Shirdi. But this doctor at Mumbai said that surgery was not required, and administrated the serum injection. Following which the swelling shrunk a lot, and the pain subsided completely. All this happened after Shri Sai Maharaj spoke those words. Thinking about it, leaves me wonderstruck and happy."

Baba asks the *sanyasi* for *dakshina*.

"On the very first day of my visit, Maharaj asked for *dakshina* from me. I replied, 'Maharaj, I am a *sanyasi* (an ascetic), where will I have money?' After I had *darshan*, Baba said this to Madhavrao Deshpande, 'स्वामी मला काही देतास का पाहिले परंतु ते कही देणार नाहीत ।। ते मजकडे आले आहेत ।। तेंव्हा मलाच त्यांना दिले पाहिजे ।।'

'I wanted to know if he would give me something. But he won't give me anything. Since he has come to me. I will give him something.'

"From the very moment these words were uttered I became trouble free. What can I say about this *Sidh Purush* (enlightened and self realised person)? Except that he is Shri Narayan in a human form."

Ref: *Sai Leela Aashad Shake 1845. Ank 5. Year 1 (1923)*

*Leela 2:*  # Nana's offering of puran polis to Baba

Baba would appear in the homes of his devotees in unique and varied *roopas* (forms) and tell them about it later. On one occasion Nana Sahib Chandorkar prepared a plate of delicious *puran polis* (chapattis with a stuffing of jaggery and gram). He brought the *naivedya* (food offerings) because he felt Baba would like the *puran polis*. When Nana arrived with the piping hot delectable *polis*, Baba had just finished His meal and was seated near the *katada* (railing).

Nonetheless Nana requested Baba to accept the *naivedya*. Baba replied, "Nana, I have just finished my meal. You leave the plate here. Go to the *wada* and have your meal." On hearing Baba's order, Nana did return to the *wada* but before leaving, he said to Madhavrao Deshpande, "You stay with Baba, and when he partakes anything from this plate, come and inform me. Only then will I eat."

True to his word Shama sat near Baba, after some time Baba said, "Has Nana had his meal?" Shama replied, "No. He will eat only after you have eaten something from his offering." Baba laughed and said, "*Arre* Shama, when he was preparing the dish for me, I took the form of a fly and ate his *naivedya*." So Shama went to the *wada* and related what Baba had said and asked Nana to have his meal.               Ref: *Sai Leela Aashad Shake 1845. Ank 5. Year 1 (1923)*

## Leela 3:       Baba teaches Nana the impact of speech

Once Baba told Nana, '*अरे कोणी आपल्या दारी मागावयाला आले तर त्याला आपल्या शक्तीप्रमाणे द्यावे आपल्या जवळ द्यावयाला नसले तर निदान त्याच्याशी गोड शब्द तरी बोलावे ।।*"

"*Arre*, if anyone comes to your door begging for alms, give them what is feasible, and according to your ability (*shakti pramane*). If you don't have anything to give, then refuse them politely and sweetly." Soon after Baba had imparted this *bodha,* Nana returned home.

About four days later, an old lady came to his door begging. The servant informed her that there was no *bhiksha* which could be given. But she obstinately stood there, insisting to be given *bhiksha*. Then Nana came and shouted at her.

A few days later, Nana went to Shirdi. Baba said, "Nana, the other day I told you to talk sweetly to anyone who came to your door for alms. You forgot that, didn't you? I came to you in the form of that old lady begging for alms. All I got was a lot of abuses from you." Nana repented and learned a valuable lesson.

Ref: *Sai Leela Aashad Shake 1845. Ank 5. Year 1 (1923)*

*Leela 4:* # Baba comes in the form of a dog

In *Shri Sai Satcharita* Chapter 3, *Ovi* 81, Baba says, "Do not repulse or reject anyone contemptuously, be it a dog, pig or common fly. No one comes to us without some special bond from previous births."

Once a sickly bitch came close to Mhalsapathy, wagging her tail. She looked very ill and was drooling from the mouth. He threw a stone at her and drove her away. She ran away yelping. Later he went for Baba's *darshan*. Baba, turning to him said, "I went with a great deal of hope to Bhakta (Baba used to call Mhalsapathy Bhakta or Bhagat) hoping for some food, but all I got was a stone thrown at me."

These *leelas* were to teach the devotees about the impact of speech. Baba often said, "अरे कोणालाही हाड हाड झिड झिड करु नये अपल्याकडे कुत्रा, मांजर कोणीही येते ते काही तरी संबंधामुळेच येते।। आपण कोणाचाही कंटाळा करु नये।।"

"Don't speak disparagingly and say *hudd hudd* or *chidd chidd* to anybody. If a cat, dog or a person comes to you, they do so because of some connection (*rinanubandh*). If anybody comes to your home, don't be listless and never ignore them." Baba didn't give lectures needlessly. With his unique *leelas* he brought into practice what he taught.            Ref: *Sai Leela Aashad Shake 1845. Ank 5. Year 1 (1923)*

## *Leela 5:*        Kaka drives away a
## dog and repents

Two hours after Baba said this, Kaka and his friends were sitting near the *wada*. A dog came and sat on the steps nearby. He drove it away; the dog ran and sat on the steps in front of him. There he was pelted with stones. The dog went away shrieking with pain, suddenly Kaka was reminded of Baba's words. Kaka with a twinge of sadness thought, 'If I had not driven the dog away, but had given him a piece of *bhakari*, he would have gone away without being hurt.'

That very evening Das Ganu did *kirtan*. The story sung there in was about Namdev. Once a dog came and took a *bhakari* from the food offering (*naivedya*) that Namdev had placed before the idol of Vitthal. Namdev said, ("*Deva!* don't eat dry *bhakari*, apply *ghee* (clarified butter) on it." Namdev, then ran after the dog with a bowl of *ghee*.

That very night Madhavrao Adkar was reading aloud the *Bhakta Leelamrut* in the *Maruti* Mandir. The portion being read was about Namdev and the dog. In this way Baba reinforced what he had taught in the morning.

Ref: *Sai Leela Aashad Shake 1845. Ank 5. Year 1 (1923)*

## Leela 6: Hansraj beats the cat and welts appear on Baba's back

Hansraj Vaani had asthma; it was very severe and tormented him day and night. He was advised by Narsinga Baba Maharaj of Nasik to seek refuge at Baba's feet. Hence he and his wife came to Shirdi and made it their home.

Baba cautioned Hansraj, and told him not to eat curd, or acidic and pungent food items. But Hansraj loved curds and felt that the meal was incomplete without it. In fact he felt, he could give up his life, rather than give up eating curd. He forced his wife to prepare curd daily, so he could have it for lunch. They had lunch after the noon *arati*, and while they attended it a cat would sneak in and eat the curd. This bothered Hansraj a lot, as he had to have the meal without it.

So he devised a plan, he asked his wife to keep the vessel in a sling and hang it from the rafter. Nonetheless, the cat somehow managed to eat it. One day he decided to catch the cat in the act and give it a good thrashing. He waited with a stick in his hand for the cat to commit the act. Indeed the cat came into the house and somehow managed to climb up and eat the curd. As soon as the cat had finished eating, she descended and Hansraj gave her a good thrashing.

In the evening Hansraj went to the Dwaraka Mai, where Baba was sitting along with his devotees. Baba looking at Hansraj said, "There is an *uptiya* (one who does the reverse of what he is asked to do) who wants to die by eating sour and pungent things, but I will not allow him to do so. I went to his home in the form of a cat to eat the curd, and he gave me a good thrashing." Then Baba exposed his back and there were red welts from the beating.

Ref: *Devotees' Experiences of Shri Sai Baba, by Narasimha Swamiji*

6

Many a time Baba appeared before his *bhaktas* (devotees) to assure and satisfy them. But he did so in unique and different *roopas* (forms).

"Sometimes I am a dog, sometimes a pig, a cow, a cat, a fly and an aquatic creature. In various forms do I move about in the universe. Know that I like only him who sees me in all living beings. So give up this sense of differentiation. This is the way to worship me," said Baba to Mrs Tarkhad when she fed a hungry dog, and then a mud splattered pig.                    Ref: *Shri Sai Satcharita, Ovi 129-130 Chapter 9*

*Leela 7:*          # Kaka Sahib prepares shira prasad for Baba

Kaka Sahib was an astute and dedicated devotee of Baba. He noticed that whenever *shira* (semolina halva) was offered as offering, Baba would make it a point to eat a little. So he decided to offer *shira* to Baba every day.

He timed all his household chores accordingly. Just before the noon *arati*, all the *prasad* would be offered. So Dixit would go to the *wada* when Baba was in Lendi Baugh, and prepare the *shira*. Indeed it was quite a chore, but Dixit prepared it with love and devotion. The *shira* was made on a kerosene oil stove; where meticulously he measured all the ingredients and made delicious *shira*. Then he took it to the Dwaraka Mai, and kept it there. Dixit would then do Baba's *charan seva* (massage Baba's feet) and *pad puja* (wash Baba's feet with water and ingest it as *tirth*). Following the *pad puja*, the *arati* would commence.

After the noon *arati* Baba sat in front of the *nimbar*, and all the *prasad* received were placed before him. Bade Baba sat along with Baba and they had lunch. If Baba took a little of the *shira* prepared by Dixit, he would be ecstatic. After taking Baba's permission, he would return to the *wada*. There he and the other devotees, who were his guests, had their lunch. Then Dixit's *shira* was given to every one as *prasad*. Every day he followed this routine.

## Dixit's wish is granted

Dixit yearned to sit along with Baba during lunch. Bade Baba was fortunate to have a seat next to Baba. Dixit felt that it was an honour, and good fortune to dine with his guru. Much later his wish came to fruition.

Every single day he read Eknath's *Bhawarth Ramayan*. In *Yudh Kand* Chapter 88, there is a story about Lord Hanuman, who longed to eat the *uchista* (leftover food) of Lord Rama. So one day Hanuman waited patiently and when Rama began eating, he jumped in front of him and picked the plate that Rama was eating from and flunged it up to the sky. Hanuman quickly leaped up, caught the plate and sat on a tree and ate the left over. Later Hanuman stood in front of Rama, the latter knowing of his utter devotion and love, laughed and joked with him.

Keeping the example of Hanuman in mind Dixit did a similar thing. One day after the *shira* was offered; he waited for Baba to start eating it. Then he went up to him and took the vessel of *shira* back to his *wada*, where he and his fellow devotees made a meal of it. Later when he came to the Dwaraka Mai, Baba laughed and joked about it. But the wonderful result was that the very next day Baba asked Dixit to sit with him for lunch.

Ref: *Sai Leela Dixit Ank. Aashad Shake 1848. Ank 6. Year 4 (1926)*

## Some little known facts about Dixit

Kaka Sahib Dixit was a Gujarati Nagar Brahmin; he was highly educated, both in the academic and the spiritual field. When he first visited Shirdi he was at the height of his profession, he had achieved in 15 years what many were unable to achieve in a lifetime. Kaka was a famous solicitor, and had a practice of his own in Mumbai.

From the moment he set eyes on Baba, Kaka knew that he must seek refuge at Baba's feet. So he visited Shirdi as often as he could. His absence from Bombay made his practice suffer, but Baba had asked him not to resign. So he visited Shirdi as frequently as he could.

8

One day he asked Baba a vital question, "Baba in the practice of law many facts are distorted, and numerous untruths are cited. These are in fact lies, what should one do in such a case." Baba replied, "Let the other lawyers say anything, but you state only the truth." This was impossible and Dixit soon left the practice of law.

Dixit passed away on the auspicious day of 11th of *Jyeshth* (July 5th 1926). He was not ailing from any disease and was fully conscious. He was talking about his *sadguru*, and with Baba's name on his lips he passed away.

That very moment at Shirdi two things happened. A huge branch of the Neem tree at Lendi Baugh broke and fell down. Secondly, there were 3 small *kalashes* (pots) on the rooftop of the Dwaraka Mai. One of them broke on its own accord. For it was often said of Dixit that he was 'stuck to the Dwaraka Mai'. Thus the Dwaraka Mai acknowledges the passing away of a beloved devotee.

## Equality of vision

Once when Baba was having his lunch, a dog came and sniffed a tumbler of buttermilk, putting his snout into it. Fakir Baba, who was seated there, summoned a boy and asked him to throw it away. While the boy was doing so, Baba said, "What is the matter?" Fakir Baba told him what had happened. Baba turning to Jog said, "Bapu, the buttermilk is good. Take it home and make *kadi* (a gravy of buttermilk) of it. Then bring it along with you in the evening, and I will eat it." This Baba ate with great relish for his supper.

Ref: *Sai Leela Chaitra Shake 1845. Ank 1. Year 1 (1923)*

## Leela 8:                     Bapuji Shastri Gulvi

A devotee named Bapuji Shastri Gulvi visited Shirdi in February 1918 for Baba's *darshan*. He had brought Ganga *jal* (water) with him, and he performed *abhishek* (holy bath) with Vedic chanting and holy rituals. After that he wanted Baba's permission to leave. He desired to go to Sajjangad for *Ramdas Navami* and participate in the festivities there. While giving him permission, Baba said, *"तेथेही आपणच आहोत व येथे ही आपणच आहोत।।"*

"I am there and I am also here." He went there and on *Ramdas Navami* at dawn he had *shakshatkar* of Baba. Not only had he met Baba but also massaged His feet for a short time, and then Baba disappeared.          Ref: *Sai Leela Chaitra Shake 1845. Ank 1. Year 1 (1923)*

## Leela 9:              Baba changes the
##                          creditor's mind

One of Baba's devotees was deep in debt. The creditor became very impatient and sent him a warrant. But the devotee didn't have the money at that time. Nor did he have any other means of procuring that amount. Nonetheless he felt calm and was confident that he would obtain the money somehow. The creditor harassed him and would wait no longer. At that time many devotees of Baba had gathered in his home. They wanted to perform *naam saptha* (continuous chanting of the name of a deity for seven days) at his home in front of Baba's portrait. The devotee gladly agreed to this and the *naam saptha* was started.

The creditor seized the opportunity, thinking that he would confiscate the debtor's home at that time. He got a 'confiscation warrant' and went there. The *naam jaap* had started and the debtor seeing the creditor went up to him and said, "It's all right, you may take anything that you desire from my home. Then I will have enough room to carry on the festivities, and *naam saptha.*" At that time Baba had such an influence on the creditor's mind that he tore up the warrant and did not send it again.

Ref: *Sai Leela Aashad Shake 1845. Ank 5. Year 1*

## *Leela 10:*  Baba smells the mogra

A friend of Kaka Sahib Dixit (unfortunately his name is not mentioned) stayed at Bandra. He performed daily *puja* to Baba's photograph. Meticulously he would dip the flower offerings in sandalwood paste and thus stick it on Baba's forehead and *charan* (feet). One day in the bunch of flowers there was a beautiful *Vat Mogra* (a type of Jasmine). The flower was very large, so he could not stick it on his forehead with sandalwood paste. Suddenly he remembered that Baba loved the smell of this flower. He lovingly took the flower to Baba's nose so that he could smell it; when it got stuck there on its own. And it remained there the whole day until the next morning.

Ref: *Sai Leela Aashad Shake 1845. Ank 5. Year 1*

## Leela 11: Shanti Kirwandikar falls in the well

Babu Kirwandikar was a Brahmin devotee staying at Shirdi. He had a three-year-old daughter called Shanti, who loved Baba a lot. She often said that she was Baba's sister, and Baba reciprocated her love and called her 'Bai'.

One day she fell into the well that was behind Sathe *wada*. It was quite a long time before they could pull her out. But she was not hurt at all. The villagers were amazed to see her hale and hearty. When they asked her about the fall, merrily she replied, "I fell into the well and my Baba held on to me for a long time. Hence I have no injuries."

Ref: *Sai Leela Aashad Shake 1845. Ank 5. Year 1 (1923)*

## Leela 12: Chidambar Keshav Gadgil pines for Baba's darshan

He was an ardent devotee of Baba, so he went to Shirdi frequently. Gadgil had a government job, and was the *chitnis* (accountant) at the Collector's office in Ahmednagar. This post he held for a long time. As Shirdi is in Ahmednagar district he was able to visit Shirdi often.

Then he got promoted to the rank of *mamlatdar* (Talluqa revenue officer) at Sinner. As Sinner is about 60 miles away from Shirdi, it was quite easy for him to come to Shirdi frequently.

12

From Sinner he got transferred to a far off place, with the order 'to join immediately'. He was saddened by the thought that he would not be able to have Baba's *darshan* frequently. The irony of all this was that the train that he boarded passed through Kopergaon. As the train halted at Kopergaon he was overwhelmed by sorrow. He thought, 'I am so close to Shirdi, yet so far as I cannot make my pilgrimage.' As the train pulled out of the station his eyes were filled with tears, and he pinned to have Baba's *darshan*.

Suddenly a small paper packet fell on him. He opened it and was surprised to find that it contained *udi*. He kept the packet safely with him. After some time he was able to go to Shirdi. There Baba said, "तू आला नाहीस म्हणून मी तुला उदी पाठविली ती पोहोचली ना?"

"Because you couldn't come I sent you a packet of *udi*. You got it? Didn't you?" Hearing these words he was filled with love and joy. He put that *udi* in a talisman and kept it with him at all times.

Ref: *Sai Leela Jyeshth Shake 1845. Ank 3. Year 1 (1923)*

"I am absolutely in the power of my devotees and stand by their side. For ever hungering after their love, and readily answering their call of distress," said Baba to Dada Bhatt, when Dr Pundit applied sandal paste on his forehead.     Ref: *Shri Sai Satcharita, Ovi 76 Chapter 11*

## Chidambar Keshav Gadgil is a Ganapathi Upasak

Gadgil was a staunch devotee of Baba, and was also an *upasak* of Lord Ganapathi. An *upasak* is a staunch devotee who strictly follows all the rituals of the chosen deity. He prayed to Baba's photograph in his home with all the rituals pertaining to Ganapathi.

On one of his visits to Shirdi, Baba was seated with some of his devotees. Baba pointing to Gadgil said, "Throw this *Mahatara* (an endearing name for a fellow devotee) out, he says that there is a rat below my *gaddi* (mattress)." Gadgil was extremely happy to hear this, for Baba had accepted his mode of doing *puja*. The rat is the *vahan* or vehicle on which Ganapathi rides.

Ref: *Sai Leela Aashad Shake 1845. Ank 5. Year 1 (1923)*

**Kirtankar deserts Nana**

Nana Sahib Chandorkar was Baba's foremost apostle. It was his habit to talk about Baba's divinity to all his friends. In fact, he spoke about Baba to any and everyone. He then brought that person to Shirdi, to meet his *sadguru*. All this he did at his own expense.

On one occasion Nana brought a *kirtankar* and his assistant with him. The *kirtankar* readily accompanied him as he had to perform *kirtans* at Ahmednagar the next day. They had Baba's *darshan*, and then Nana asked him for permission to leave. Baba asked him to have his lunch first. Nana asked the *kirtankar* and his assistant to join him, but the *kirtankar* was in a great hurry as he did not want to miss the train. If he did miss the train he would be late for the *kirtan*, hence lose a lot of money. So he and his assistant left.

Baba said, *"पहा, कसे लोक मतलबी असतात वेळ आली म्हणजे साथीदाराला सोडून आपल्या मतलबाला दक्ष असतात म्हणून आपण असा साथी करावा की, जे आपल्याला कल्पतीही सोडणार नाही।।"*

"See how conniving people are, they just look out for their own gains. If things don't go their way, they do not hesitate and leave that person in the lurch. So you should make such a friend who will not desert you. A friend who cannot even think of leaving you even in his remotest thought."

This made Nana think of such a friend, and all he would think of was his *sadguru*. Who else would think of forsaking you ever? So if you have a friend let him be Baba. Nana further states, "Have a loving relationship with everyone, but let the *sadguru* be your best friend." In *Shri Sai Satcharita* Chapter 2, Dixit asks Baba for permission to leave. The conversation takes a turn and Baba says if you take a guide with you then there is no fear of getting lost. He says,

14

"वाटाड्याबरोबर असला म्हणजे काही पंचाईत नाही मग वाघ बाजुला होऊन जातात, रीस बाजुला होऊन जातात।। नाही तर एक मोठी खाई आहे।। त्यांना वाटूं लागले।।"

"If you take a guide then there is no difficulty. You won't lose your way. The tiger will move away. The bear will move away."

So clasp the feet of the *sadguru* with love and devotion, he will help you cross the ocean of life without any difficulties.

Ref: *Sai Leela Vaishak Shake 1845. Ank 3. Year 1 (1923)*

## Leela 14: Bapu Sahib Jog performs the last rites of his mother at Shirdi

Shakaram Hari alias Bapu Sahib Jog's mother died in Shirdi. He wanted to perform the ceremonies with all the religious rituals. He decided to go to Nasik, as the Brahmins from his *shake* (caste and creed) were not available at Shirdi. He went to Baba and asked for permission to go to Nasik, and find out if the Brahmins would be available on that particular date. But Baba kept putting it off. In desperation Bapu Sahib said, "Come what may, I have to go today. There are no Brahmins from my caste here." Baba said, "We will decide about this in the evening."

In less than an hour since Baba had spoken these words, an extremely learned Vedic Brahmin from Jog's caste came to have Baba's *darshan*. He later performed the ceremony to Jog's satisfaction. So there was no reason for him to go to Nasik. Kaka Dixit was present when Jog was asking for permission. Kaka said, "Baba, let us – you, Bapu Sahib and me – go along. We will leave Jog at Nasik, then you and I will go to Mumbai." Pat came the reply, *"मी कधी कोणाला सोडणार माणूस नाही।।"*

"*Mee kadi konnala soodnar manush naahi.*" (Roughly translated – I never ever desert anybody, I am not such a person.) Baba in his typical manner had given an ordinary conversation such extraordinary meaning.

Ref: *Sai Leela Aashad Shake 1845. Ank 5. Year 1 (1923)*

## Leela 15:   Shankar Rao Ksheersagar gives all his money as dakshina

Shankar Ksheersagar was a *Mamlatdar*. Once he visited Shirdi and had Baba's *darshan* . Baba asked him for *dakshina* ; Shankar placed all the money that he had in Baba's hand. Then he happily went to the *wada*. A devotee who had seen him give *dakshina,* said, "You emptied your pocket, how will you make the return journey? You have no money left!" Calmly he replied, "Baba will provide for me."

That very evening the post master from Rahatha came to Shirdi with a relative of his. Some years ago the post master's relative had borrowed Rs 20 from Shankar. Upon meeting Shankar the relative on his own accord returned the money. Thus he had enough money to meet his expenses.

Ref: *Sai Leela Aashad Shake 1845. Ank 5. Year 1 (1923)*

## Leela 16:   Baba reads his thoughts

A friend (name not given) of Kaka Dixit came to Shirdi. He had Baba's *darshan*, and a short while later he on his own accord started massaging Baba's feet. After some time Baba said "Do not massage my feet, sit away from me." The friend did so, but his eyes filled with tears.

After some time he started massaging Baba's feet again, and Baba did not object this time. After doing namaskar they returned to the *wada*. The friend then told Kaka about the incident. "Baba is truly an *antaryami* (lives in every being). When I first started massaging Baba's feet, he allowed me to do so. Then my mind started wandering and strayed elsewhere. I thought ill of a fellow devotee, which he at once read and asked me to move away from him. When I realised what had happened, I repented and mentally asked Baba to forgive me. He did so and allowed me to massage his feet again."

Ref: *Sai Leela Aashad Shake 1845. Ank 5. Year 1 (1923)*

## Leela 17: The yellow pitambar for his samadhi

Two days after Baba took *mahasamadhi* (left his mortal body), he gave a dream vision to Moreshwar Pradhan's sister-in-law at their home at Santa Cruz.

'In your trunk you have a yellow *pitambar* (a shawl usually 2.5 metres long), sent this *pitambar* to Shirdi so that my *samadhi* (here *samadhi* is Baba's tomb) can be covered with it.' Indeed she did have a *pitambar* in her trunk. She had bought it a long time ago and had forgotten about it. Early next morning she told Pradhan about her dream. They went immediately to the trunk and sent the *pitambar* to Shirdi. Upon receiving it, the *samadhi* was covered with it. And it was used for a long time. Ref: *Sai Leela Aashad Shake 1845. Ank 5. Year 1*

**Leela 18:**     # The 30th day of his mahasamadhi

One day, early in the morning, Lakshmanrao alias Kaka Mahajani had a vivid dream. In that dream Baba said, *"निजलास काय ।। आज माझा तिसावा दिवस आहे तो कर ।।"*

"Are you asleep? Get up, it's the 30th day after my *mahasamadhi*." Mahajani got up at once and he thought that a month had passed some time ago. So he counted the days on the calendar, and indeed it was the 30th day post *Mahasamadhi*. He called the pundits and held a *puja*. The pundits performed *abhishek* of Baba's *padukas* (holy foot wear) with proper ritual, this was followed by a grand meal. He had invited many of his friends and Baba's devotees. Thus the first monthly anniversary of Baba's *punyatithi* was started. He continued to celebrate the anniversary each and every month there after at his residence in Mumbai.     *Ref: Sai Leela Aashad Shake 1845. Ank 5. Year 1*

**Leela 19:**     # Ganesh Govind Narke's letter to Kaka Dixit

This letter gives a great deal of insight into the human quality of Baba's divinity. At times he chose to be very stubborn; with 'mood swings' and often exhibited sham rage. These dramatic moods were a means to an end or to emphasise, and drive home a point. It also shows the deep *rinanubandhic* ties that Tatya Kote Patil had with

18

Baba. The ease with which they interacted with each other on a personal level.

I quote:

Two days ago on March 2nd 1918 it was *Nathshrusti* (the *punyatithi* or death anniversary of Eknath Maharaj). Many of the devotees had brought their books along, for Baba's blessings. *Aajibai* (elderly lady is called grandmother with respect) in a very melodious voice sang the *charita* (life story) of Eknath from one of those books. After Baba had breakfast, he narrated many parables and stories. Most of the stories were about Namdev and Kabir. The day was very enjoyable.

In the evening, at supper (*bhakari chi vaali*), Baba got extremely angry with Tatya. He flung the plate of *bhakari* and other dishes. Fakir Baba and Dr Pillai came to see what had happened. Baba said, "Drive him away from here or I will go away from here." In the fit of rage he ran towards Tatya as if to hit him. Baba kept shouting at Tatya all the time. Tatya went and sat in the *sabhamandap*. Then Tatya said, "Unless you eat the fruit offered, I won't let you go to the *Chavdi*."

At 7.45 p.m. the bell rang to summon the devotees, who gathered in the *sabhamandap*. They started doing *bhajans*. Tatya continued to be offended. So Baba sent Dada to call Tatya. Tatya however could not be pacified, and neither would Baba eat the fruit. By that time it was already 10.30 p.m. The *sabhamandap* was packed to suffocation with devotees. The *palki* was decorated and ready, the horse was bedecked with trinkets and standing at the entrance.

Baba went and sat near the *Nimbar*, and was calm. However, he did not speak to anyone. At that time the *palki* would proceed at Paithan, so the devotees in Shirdi started dancing and there was much merriment.

At 11 p.m. Dada asked Baba for permission to go home. Baba replied, "Where are you going? Sit down." All the while the *bhajans* were going on, everyone was extremely happy. At last Tatya gave up his stubbornness but Baba stubbornly said, "I won't go to the *Chavdi*." Then he told Dada to go home as it was very late at night. Following this Baba flew into a rage, he shouted at every one using abusive language. Then he sent every one home to have their dinner.

19

At midnight he asked for the bell to be rung. Soon all the devotees assembled in the *sabhamandap*. Then with great merriment the procession went to the *Chavdi*, and that was exactly the time of Eknath's *punyatithi*.

The next day everyone was talking about Baba's way of getting things done. At Baba's *durbar* also the same topic was discussed. Then Tatya came and stood near the wall and said, "Baba, if you had told us to do *bhajans* after midnight we would have done so? You did not have to make a show of all this rage. You are really very playful!"

Then Baba said, "You are playful. You and Bapu Sahib play all the time." He then went to Lendi Baugh, and upon returning he asked the devotees, "Why was the procession to *Chavdi* so late yesterday? Never mind, it really is joyful here."

Ref: *Sai Leela Aashad Shake 1845. Ank 5. Year 1*


Leela 20:        # Ya Ramdas

## (Come Ramdas)

Once Dixit and a friend of his went to Shirdi. When they went for *darshan*, Baba looked at his friend and said, "Ya Ramdas!" (Come Ramdas). Later, Dixit inquired, "Why did Baba say, 'come Ramdas'. There must be some reason." The friend could not think of any reason for a long time. Suddenly he found the reason and said, "About two years ago I started doing Ram *jaap* mentally. But no one knows about it, I did not even tell my wife let alone other people. But Baba being an *antaryami* knew about this." Baba in his own way strengthened his faith in the mantra he had chosen. He continued doing it as Baba had approved of it.

Ref *Sai Leela Chaitra Shake 1845. Ank 1. Year 1 (1923)*

## Leela 21:

# Appa Kulkarni is charged with embezzling

Appa Kulkarni was a resident of Shirdi. He was an ardent devotee of Baba. Once the villagers accused him of embezzling money from the village accounts. Then they reported the matter to the officer in charge. A few days later, Appa received 'summons' from him. Appa was extremely frightened, so he ran to Baba and told him everything. Baba told him that the officer at present was at Nevasa. So he should go there. And before appearing in front of the officer, he should first pray to Shri Mohiniraj (Vishnu took the form of a female, called Mohini).

Appa followed Baba's advice and did exactly what he was told. There he appeared before the officer and pleaded his innocence. The officer said, "I don't think you embezzled the money", and let him go. Appa danced with joy and thanked Baba all the way home. As soon as he reached Shirdi he went and told Baba everything, thanking him from the bottom of his heart. Baba said, "God is the doer. And he can make the impossible, possible."

Ref: *Sai Leela Chaitra Shake 1845. Ank 1. Year 1 (1923)*

## Do not ask for udi to patch up old clothes

Some days after Appa was acquitted of the charges of embezzlements, he came to the Dwaraka Mai to sit and chat with Baba. Baba casually said, "Appa, thieves have come to our village. They are not ordinary thieves for they don't steal anything tangible from the house. Their eyes are set on the most valuable part of one's wealth. What is interesting is that no one can catch them in the act of stealing. They will attack you first. So go and make proper arrangements." Appa couldn't understand what Baba meant by this. He immediately hired some *Bhils* to protect his property.

That night Appa got cramps in his abdomen, followed by incessant vomiting and loose motions. He had contracted cholera, which rapidly had become precarious. His eyes were sunken and his pulse became feeble. Appa's wife got frightened, she ran to Baba and started crying. She told Baba that her husband was dying, and asked him for *udi*.

Baba replied, "Do not grieve. Death waits for every one. Birth and death are the acts of the Almighty. No one lives and dies here. If you look at it with the eyes of knowledge, you will realise that no one is different. When the clothes become old and frayed you throw them away. In the same way the soul which is immortal, casts off the worn out body. Do not, therefore, ask for *udi* to patch up old rags. Do not stop him, let him go. He has reached his life's goal. He will go to heaven. Right now he is changing his clothes in front of me." Baba sent her home and soon after Appa died. She was very sad but comforted by Baba's words.

The next day a couple of people died of Cholera. The villagers were frightened, they begged Baba to stop this scourage from spreading. Baba said, "Only 7 people will die and after that Shirdi will be rid of cholera." Of course Baba's prediction came true.

Ref: *Shri Bhakta Leelamrut by Das Ganu*

## Baba's thoughts on death and dying

Nana Sahib Chandorkar was indeed fortunate to be in close contact with Baba. Often they had long conversations on various subjects. Nana called these conversations 'Baba's *updesh*'.

Baba spoke thus:

"As long as life exists one must take good care of one's body. But one should not weep over death. After death nothing exists for you to cry over. Wise men are not moved by death. It is the foolish who give vent to their feelings in times of death.

"The body until death is a loan from the 5 elements, which the lifeforce repays. On full and final payment of the loan, air mixes with air, and fire with fire. Thus the 5 elements go to their final places. The body belongs to the earth, and its loss is not a matter of mourning.

"Similarly, the birth of a child need not be the cause for rejoicing, as birth is as natural a phenomenon as death. One must simply stay calm, i.e., unmoved by birth and death.

"The earth bears the seed, the clouds water it and the sun helps the seed to germinate. When the seed germinates, do the earth, the clouds and the sun rejoice and start dancing? Whether the sprout turns into a big tree or it dries up and withers is something that should cause neither rejoicing nor sorrow. If we act in this manner, how can there be misery or cause for lamentation? The state of absolution is the absence of misery and lamentation."

Ref: *Shri Bhakta Leelamrut by Das Ganu*

## Leela 22: Kondaji Sutar's hay stack catches fire

Kondaji was devoted to Baba, and he lived in Shirdi. His love and devotion for Baba was intense. Baba reciprocated and called him Kondya.

One afternoon Kondya was sitting in the Dwaraka Mai with Baba. Suddenly Baba said, "Go to the Khalwadi (the place where harvest is threshed) as your stack of wheat is burning. You better go there." It was summer and scorching hot. The barn had a multitude of hay stacks that were drying in midday sun, and were ready for threshing. Kondaji ran to his barn and looked around but could not detect any smoke or fire. He returned after checking each and every hay stack.

Kondaji said, "Baba, why did you send me there needlessly in this heat? I checked every stack, and they are all right." At that very moment there was a strong gust of wind. Then Baba said, "Turn around and see the smoke rising from your granary. The central stack is on fire."

He turned around and saw one of the hay stacks on fire. Frightened out of his wits, he believed that all the hay stacks would soon be reduced to ashes. The wind started blowing with vigour. Anguished at seeing the smoke bellowing from his granary, Kondya ran to the Khalwadi shouting for help. By this time the other farmers also saw what had happened, frightened and distraught they ran to the Dwaraka Mai.

## Baba saves the entire harvest from burning

The villagers pleaded with Baba and asked him to save their hay stacks. "Baba, our hay stacks will be the next to burn. Please put out the fire, or all the granaries will burn. We will incur great losses and will go hungry," they said in unison. The compassionate Baba went to the barn and took some water and poured it around the burning stack. He made a circle of water around the central stack. "Let this central stack burn. Do not try to extinguish it. It's an offering to *Agni dev*. Nothing will happen to the rest of the stacks," said Baba. And so it came to pass.

The devotees learned a valuable lesson of making an offering to *Agni dev* (the fire god to whom food offerings are made daily), the sustainer of life. Baba had control over the five elements: earth, wind, fire, ether and rain. His word was law unto them.

Ref: *Sai Leela Chaitra Shake 1845. Ank1. Year 1 (1923)*

"The sense of ownership is the root cause of joy and sorrow, " says Baba.

That evening Nana Sahib Chandorkar went to the Dwaraka Mai for Baba's *darshan*. Baba said, "O ! Nana, look at these greedy people. Today Kondaji's central stack of wheat burned down. Now he is mourning his loss. Gain and loss, birth and death are all under god's control. But these foolish people do not realise this. They dance with joy when they get capital gains and cry bitterly when there is a loss.

"Joy and sorrow come from a sense of ownership. It is ignorance to claim ownership. The stack that burnt did not belong to the Marwadi in the first place. The hay consisted of seeds that were sown in the earth. The clouds watered them and the sun kneaded them into shape. Thus the earth, the cloud and the sun are the real owners. All the things in this world are thus produced.

"Nana go and ask the Marwadi why he is weeping over the loss of something that was never his. The Lord gives with one hand and he takes with the other. It is this sense of ownership that is the root cause of joy and sorrow." Ref: *Shri Bhakta Leelamrut by Das Ganu*

## Leela 23:  Nana Sahib Bere escapes being attacked by dacoits

Nana Sahib worked as an inspector in the Agricultural Department, and was an ardent devotee of Baba. On one of his visits to Shirdi, Baba said, "You should leave right away. Hurry and do not delay. Go directly to Kopergaon station and stay there."

The other devotees said, "What is the need to hurry like this, as there is plenty of time for the train to arrive." Nonetheless, he did not waste any time. He hired a *tonga* right away, and asked the driver to hurry. They overtook another *tonga* on the way and reached the station safely. After a long time the occupants of the other *tonga* reached the station. They were battered and bruised.

Upon inquiring about this, they told him that they were waylaid by dacoits. The dacoits stole all their money and thrashed them mercilessly. Bere mentally thanked Baba for the timely protection.

Ref: *Sai Leela Chaitra Shake 1845. Ank 1. Year 1*

*Leela 24:* ## This devotee sends dakshina to Baba along with penalty

A householder (his name is not mentioned) along with a friend of his visited Shirdi in 1910. The friend took care of all the expenses to and from Shirdi. The householder took three coins of one rupee denomination with him. But he was determined not to give any to Baba. Baba, however, did not ask him for any. The *darshan* had a profound effect on him. When they reached Bandra where he resided, he told his friend, "I took three coins with me and I am bringing them back with me."

The next day his wife had a vivid dream in which she saw her husband's purse containing the three coins along with two match boxes lying in the bathroom. The dream was so vivid that she went to the bathroom to look for herself. When her husband got up, she narrated the dream to him. The husband put his hand in his pocket and indeed the three articles were there.

The householder learnt his lesson so he sent those three rupees along with twelve *annas* as penalty. That is four *annas* for each rupee. Later this householder along with his family went and stayed for a month in Shirdi.        Ref: *Sai Leela Chaitra Shake 1845. Ank 1. Year 1 (1923)*

# Lakshman K Nulkar
                       # is relieved of his eye disease

Lakshman K Nulkar alias Tatya Sahib was an ardent devotee of
Baba. Once he had an eye problem. The eye hurt a lot and he
had 'double vision'. Whatever he looked at or read, he saw two of
them. So he took leave and along with a friend sought medical advice
and treatment. As *Gurupurnima* was only a few days away he decided
to visit Shirdi. Since he had decided to stay only for a couple of days
he did not bring any medicines with him. The day he reached Shirdi
his eyes hurt a lot. The next day Baba said, "Shama, today my eyes
are hurting a great deal", and from that moment Nulkar's eyes started
healing. After some time his eyes were back to normal.

Ref: *Sai Leela Chaitra Shake 1845. Ank 1. Year 1 (1923)*


*Leela 26:*                    # Mr Curtis visits Shirdi

In *Shri Sai Satcharita* Chapter 11, *Ovi* 21, the incident of an
'English gentleman' is given, unfortunately his name is not
mentioned. He probably was Mr Curtis; his visit to Shirdi is narrated
below.

Once Bapu Sahib Jog, Bala Sahib Bhate and Dev were awaiting
the arrival of Bhau Sahib Dixit who was on his way to Shirdi. Baba
said rather vehemently, "साला हमारे को देखने आया है । पर हम तो नंगा फकीर है ।"

*"Saale, hamare ko dekhne yaaye hai. Per hum thoo nanga fakir hai."* (Roughly translated – *Saale* (an abuse), they are coming to see me. I am but a naked Fakir.) When he said this Baba was fully dressed. They wondered at Baba's words.

At that time an entourage consisting of Mr Curtis, who was the commissioner, his wife, Mr Macmillan (Collector of the district), his assistant Bhau Sahib Joglekar , were entering the boundary of Shirdi. They passed the Dwaraka Mai and proceeded to the *Chavdi*. Seeing this entourage, Jog and his friends understood Baba's words.

Joglekar sent one of his peons to bring Bala Bhate. But Bhate was disinclined to meet them. He and his friends decided to wait for Dixit and then all of them would go to the *Chavdi*. Just at that time Baba told them to go home, have their bath and daily rituals, and then go to meet the entourage. They did exactly what Baba had said.

With the 'entourage', Bhate and his friends went to the Dwaraka Mai. As Baba was returning from his *bhiksha* rounds, Mrs Curtis went to Baba, and said she would like to speak to him for a few minutes. "Wait for half an hour," said Baba. Then Baba went to the Dwaraka Mai. Mrs Curtis followed him and tried again. "Wait for an hour," said Baba. But as Mr Curtis was in a hurry to go, she had to leave with the entourage. As she could not speak to Baba her wish could not be fulfilled. Here Baba uses the word naked which does not mean nude, but as the saying goes 'I am naked, I have nothing to give you.'          Ref: *Sai Leela Vaishak Shake 1845. Ank 1. Year 1 (1923)*

## Leela 27:   Baba asks Nana Sahib Dengle what the birds are saying

In *Shri Sai Satcharita* Chapter 15, a lizard clicks excitedly and happily, awaiting the arrival of her sister from Aurangabad. It happens that a lizard comes, with a devotee from Aurangabad in the mouth bag of his horse, and runs and meets her sister. Baba answers the devotee when questioned about the click of the lizard, "The lizard is overcome with joy that her sister is coming here to meet her from Aurangabad." Be it the clicking of a lizard or the twittering of birds Baba knew and heard everything.

### Baba goes to Nana Sahib's home

Nana Sahib Dengle was an ardent devotee of Baba. He loved Baba intensely and Baba would go to his home in Nigoj off and on. They would sit under the Neem tree, and chat for some time. Then Baba would return to Shirdi taking the main road, after that walk through the village and go to the Dwaraka Mai.

One day Baba in great haste went to Nigoj early in the morning. Dengle was pleasantly surprised to see him. He made Baba sit comfortably in the courtyard, and then joined him. A few hours later, some birds perched on a tree nearby started twittering excitedly. Nana fell silent and listened to them. Baba knew that Nana could understand bird language. Baba said, "Nana, what are the birds saying?"

Dengle was silent because he knew Baba's power. Baba knew the past, present and future, let alone what the birds were saying. But because Baba asked him, he replied, "They say that nine people will die in Shirdi today." At once Baba hired a *tonga* and returned to Shirdi. At Shirdi the villagers were happily preparing *prasad* for *Shani dev*. They had a big *handi* (copper pot) ready. All the villagers had assembled there to partake of it.

**Baba asks Bhagoji Shinde to throw the prasad on the floor**

Baba, however, went straight to the Dwaraka Mai and sent a messenger to fetch Bhagoji Shinde immediately. Bhagoji came at once and Baba said, "Go to the *Shani* Mandir at once and throw all the *prasad* on the floor." Bhagoji was astounded to hear this but as Baba had commanded him, he did just that. Hurriedly he carried out the task and ran back to the Dwaraka Mai and took shelter at Baba's feet.

As expected the villagers ran to the Dwaraka Mai and angrily complained to Baba of the sacrilegious act committed by Bhagoji. Baba calmly said, "I ordered him to do so, now go and see what is in the *prasad*." Confused, they ran to the scene and taking a big ladle swirled the *prasad* around only to find a dead serpent in it. Trembling with fear they came to the Dwaraka Mai and prostrated before Baba. They thanked him for saving the whole village from utter calamity and death.

*Leela 28:* # Vasudev Sadashiv Joshi sees Lord Narasimha in Baba's photograph

Joshi was very fond of having *darshan* of saints and *sadgurus*. He had the good fortune of meeting Sai Maharaj. Chidambar Keshev alias Anna Sahib Gadgil had started an *annadan* centre in Gangapur. He purchased the grains and groceries from Sholapur, and it was there that he met Joshi on a business level. Later they became dear friends, as they were 'like-minded' people.

One day Joshi received a letter from Gadgil saying that he was at Shirdi for some days, so Joshi should avail of this opportunity and join him there. He further added that the fare, to and fro from Shirdi, was ten rupees. And it was worth spending. If he did so Shri Narayan would give him a million in return. Joshi was touched by his letter, so he left immediately.

Upon reaching Shirdi he was accommodated in Sathe *wada*. He was extremely happy to see Gadgil there, who had made all the necessary arrangements. Then he had Baba's *darshan* and was filled with bliss. Upon returning to Sathe *wada*, Joshi saw a 40 x 50-inch photograph of Baba in the *wada*. Twice a day, *arati* was performed to it. Another photograph of Baba was in Dixit *wada*, and here too *arati* was performed twice a day. The photograph in Sathe *wada* held his attention and he could not take his eyes off it.

At the evening *arati*, while looking at Baba in the photograph, he saw Lord Narasimha. He looked at that *roopa* with great concentration, and soon became oblivious of his surroundings. The *arati* was over, and he was oblivious of it, then his friend Gadgil shook him and asked him to accompany him to the *wada*. This *leela* occurred during the *arati* for three consecutive days. Then he could not contain himself, so he told his friends about it. They told him that Baba often does such *leelas*.

But the *leela* left an indelible mark on him. Soon he felt his soul stirring, and perceived the presence of the Lord in each and every particle of matter. He also felt that he should pray without any selfish motives because God knows his wants and gives what he needs. Thus he felt that his pilgrimage to Shirdi was very fruitful.

Ref: *Sai Leela Chaitra Shake 1845. Ank. 1. Year 1 (1923)*

## Vasudev Joshi asks Baba for permission to return home

Filled with utter bliss and serene calm Joshi had to return home. He thanked Sathe for the hospitality extended by him. Sathe, then informed him that, without Baba's permission, it would be impossible to leave Shirdi. The other *Sevakaris* (volunteers) advised him to ask Baba for some wish to be granted. Joshi replied, "I came here for the sole purpose of having Baba's *darshan* without any other wish or motive. So I am disinclined to ask him for anything. After a long time I got a chance to meet Baba, and my desire and wish is fulfilled." They then urged him to ask Baba to bless his company. It was called Shri Satyanarayan Company. Vasudev was unconvinced by their pleas.

At about 2 o'clock that day Vasudev along with Gadgil and his relatives went to meet Baba. Nonetheless his companions asked Baba to bless his business without mentioning name. *"यांना नारायणांनी चटणी भाकरीस काही कमी केलं आहे काय, त्यांची इच्छा नसता तुम्ही बळजबरी का करता।।"*

*"Yana Narayanani chutney bhakari sa kahi kaami kele aahey kaay? Thyana vichara va thyanchi icchaya nasthan tumhi baaljaabri ka karath asae."* (Roughly translated – Has Lord Narayan not given him chutney and *bhakari*? Ask him if he lacks anything? Why are you forcing him to ask for something, when he has no desire to do so?) The group was amazed to hear Baba say exactly what was in Joshi's mind.

Ref: *Sai Leela Chaitra Shake 1845. Ank. 1. Year 1 (1923)*

## Baba gives Joshi burfi and salted peanuts

Later when Joshi asked Baba for permission to return home, Baba said, *"निरपेक्ष जिवांना येण्याची व जाण्याची परवानगीची जरूरी नाही . त्यानी वाटेल त्या वेळी यावे व वाटेल त्या वेळी जावे।।"*

"Such a person, without any ulterior motive, or desire of gain, does not need to ask for permission. You may come and go whenever your heart desires." Then Baba gave each of them a piece of *burfi*. The rest of the group felt that three pieces of *burfi prasad* would not be sufficient for distribution at home. So Joshi decided to buy eight *annas* worth of *burfi* from some shop, as he believed that any *prasad* bought in Shirdi was Baba's *prasad*.

He set out to buy the *prasad*, when he saw a man carrying a platter full of *burfi*. The man told him that Baba had sent him specially to give the *prasad* to Gadgil's friend, i.e., Joshi. So they divided the *prasad* amongst themselves.

That day Shirdi had its 'Sunday Bazaar' when neighbouring villagers came to sell their produce at the central market. The group wanted salted peanuts for the way home. They bought some from a villager who was on her way to the market. As it was delicious, Gadgil gave a person a rupee and asked him to buy some from the market. Sathe met him on the way and asked him where he was going? "To buy some peanuts for Joshi and his group," he replied. No sooner had he uttered these words, Baba sitting in the Dwaraka Mai said, "Take two big baskets of salted peanuts and give them to

Gadgil and his friends. The rest, distribute to the devotees seated here." Some devotee had, a while ago, brought two sacks of salted peanuts and offered them to Baba. The group was amazed at Baba's omnipresence and omniscience. Joshi and the group returned to Sholapur with tears of joy in their eyes.

Ref: *Sai Leela. Chaitra Shake 1845. Ank 1. Year 1 (1923)*

## Baba consents to let his photograph be taken

Joshi returned to Sholapur in a state of utmost calm, peace and bliss. His devotion for Baba increased manifold. There he met the owner of V S Photographers, his name is not mentioned. He was totally devoted to Baba. This photographer had taken a photograph of Baba, which he had given to Joshi a while ago. Joshi venerated that photograph daily, and prayed to it.

One day Joshi told the photographer to take a trip to Shirdi, and take a photograph of Baba for him. He also gave him a letter, addressed to Gadgil, requesting him to make arrangements for his stay. Then he gave him money for all the expenses he would incur on the trip.

The photographer went to Shirdi, and had Baba's *darshan*. Then he sat in front of him. After some time Baba said, "अरे तुला सत्यनारायन कंपनीचे जोशी बुवांनी फोटो घेण्यास पाठिविले आहे ना, मग बसलास कां तुला पाहिजे तसा फोटो घे।।"

"*Arre, tula Satyanarayan companicha Joshi Bua ne photo ghanyasa patvile aaheth magg baslas ka tula kasla pahighe taasa phoyo ghee.*" (Roughly translated – *Arre*, didn't Joshi Bua of Satyanarayan company send you to take a photograph? Then why are you just sitting there? Take a photograph in any pose that you want.) Then without any hesitation, Baba with a great deal of joy and happiness sat and allowed his photograph to be taken. Then he stood up and allowed the photographer to take one more photograph.

When the photographer was leaving after a four day stay, Baba said, "तु फोटोची किंमत वाजवी पेक्षा जास्त घेऊ नको, बाकी तू सत्यनारायन कंपनीच्या जोशी बुवांचा पट्टिशिष्य आहेस ते तुला किंमत कधी ही जास्त देऊ देणार नाहीत व त्यांच्या अर्शिवादने तुझे कल्याण होणार आहेत ।।"

"When you sell these photographs, do not charge more than the cost price. You are the disciple of Joshi Bua of Satyanarayan Company; he will never ever let you sell it for a profit. By the blessings of Joshi Bua you will get spiritual upliftment and emancipation."

Then Baba gave him permission to leave. At Sholapur they registered the photographs under the name of *Bhiksha Sanstha*. They received many orders for those photographs, and were able to recover the expenses of the Shirdi trip, and much more. This is the *leela* of 'Baba's photograph with consent.'

Ref: *Sai Leela Chaitra Shake 1845. Ank 1. Year 1 (1923)*

## Leela 29:       M B Rege meets his master

Rege was spiritually inclined from a very young age. His family deity was Shanta Durga of Goa, and he was devoted to her. After his thread ceremony, he started praying to Shri Vishnu with a great deal of devotion and concentration. Along with this, he practiced yoga and meditation.

In 1910 he had several 'out of body' experiences and dream visions. In the first one he saw himself lying on his bed, while he was disconnected from the body. There in front of him stood Vishnu. About an hour later he again saw Vishnu with another figure. 'This is Sai Baba of Shirdi, He is your man, and you must resort to Him,' said Vishnu.

In his third dream vision he was travelling in space. Then he passed over a small village. He was told that the village was Shirdi. He asked a person, "Is there anyone called Sai Baba here?" The person replied in the affirmative, and took him to the Masjid, and there ended the dream vision.

Rege first visited Shirdi in 1910, there he went to the Dwaraka Mai. Baba was seated with both his legs outstretched; Rege placed his head on his feet. After an initial rebuff Baba beckoned him to come near him. Rege went and laid his head on Baba's feet.

Baba hugged him and said, "You are my child. When strangers are around we keep the children away." Rege perceived the deep love that Baba had and he responded. After that Rege visited Shirdi whenever he could.

*Leela 30:*   # Rege meets the divine mother Radha Krishna Mai

Baba asked Rege to go and stay with Radha Krishna Mai. A whole book can be written about this incredible devotee. The adjectives used to do so will not convey an iota of her worth. So I will quote from a letter written by Rege.

"On my first visit, the Master (Baba) asked me to go to mother Radha Krishna, whom he (Baba) described as 'his mother and mine'. My association with her has been very fulfilling and I owe my spiritual life to her. I had no doubt in my mind that she was the *yoga maya* like the *yogini* who gave Shri Ramkrishna Paramahamsa his training in *tantra*.

"Mother Radha Krishna, whom the Master always referred to as Rama Krisni, was to me an ideal of the *madhur bhakti* of the *gopis*. All her belongings in the world were a durrie (cotton mat), a blanket, a pair of dhotis, Eknath Maharaj's *Bhagwat*, and a *lota* (a small vessel). She had an idol of Lord Krishna whom she called 'Chhabi', like Ramlala of Shri Ramkrishna. She treated the Chhabi like a child and fondly worshipped it. Her time was spent in the service of the Master and Chhabi. Some times she would sing *bhajans* and become unconscious, and fall into a deep trance.

"The devotees I met at Shirdi had views of their own regarding *bhakti* and each one or a group thought that his or their own way was the right one, and very often there was intolerance of the other view. Mother Radha Krishna thought that the Master should, like the idols at Tirupati, Mathura, Dwaraka and Pandharpur, have good clothes, ornaments, *palki* and *rath*. Other devotees like Das Ganu, Dabolkar and many more thought that Baba was a fakir and ostentations were against his creed.

"Once when a velvet coat was being put on Baba, he refused to have it. The devotees got credence to their view and thought that it was the right and only view."

Thanks to her, we devotees are enjoying the *Chavdi* procession, the *rath* and *palki* procession till today.

## Das Ganu acknowledges Mai's madhur bhakti

Rege continues in his letter, and I quote,

"Das Ganu was a great devotee, and we find in his *kirtans* the reference to the love of *gopis*. But he probably thought that what was proper for Lord Krishna was not so for a fakir. Being confined to the residence and in company of the mother, I was far away from Das Ganu until after the Master's *Mahasamadhi*. He then came to Indore and stayed with me. Then with tears in his eyes he said, 'Bala Sahib, you are very fortunate to have a devotee of the highest order in *madhur bhakti*. I do *kirtans* on Mirabai, Janabai and the *gopis*, and tears flow from my eyes, but I could not appreciate the *madhur bhakti* of Radha Krishna Mai in real life.'"

## Rege practices Yoga

"In 1911, I thought of practicing yoga, so I invoked my Master as I wanted no other Guru. Riling on the story of Ekalavya, who got *shastra* and *astra vidya* from a mud image of Dronacharya, I began *asana* and *pranayam* sitting before the picture of my Master. I could control my breath and stop five to six beats of my heart in about a year's time. Once in 1912, talking of yoga and control of bodily functions, the Mother told me that she had succeeded in stopping her monthly periods!"

## Mai had an iron will and strength of a giant

"Mother Radha Krishna was of ordinary built, i.e., about five feet tall, but had an iron will and the strength of a giant. She would fetch water from a well about a furlong away in large pots, which she picked up without anyone's help, when even a strong man would need the help of another for this purpose. She once gave me a blow on my chest and said, 'You are a *samsari* (worldly person)! Is this hollow?'

"She then asserted that she was stronger than me. I replied that I was only a child. She then suggested a trial of strength, and insisted on it, in spite of my refusal. The road leading to Rahatha would be deserted in the afternoon and she suggested that we run with the other on the back. I told her to get on my back and I would run first. I ran about two furlongs and she said she was satisfied, and said I may stop. She then had me get on her back, and ran more than two furlongs, and asked whether she was not the stronger. I said it was doubtlessly so. Then she asked me to get off her back. I said I was happy on the back of my Mother. She threatened to throw me off her back. I replied that the world would laugh if a fond mother did so.

"Eventually I got a promise from her that she would carry me on her back on the spiritual path. It appears that this was preordained by the Master. For when we returned to Mother's residence, I was called by Baba and asked what we were doing. When I told him everything and Mother's promise, the Master said, 'She surely will take you on her back and so will I.' Then he directed me to give up the practice of Yoga. 'Do *bhakti*, nothing more is necessary. Only let your heart, head and hand be one' (He pointed to the head, heart and hand – let these be one.)"

## Mother hates publicity

"Mother Radha Krishna hated publicity. A gentleman from Bombay took some snapshots of her without her knowledge; but someone spoke of it just as the man was leaving Shirdi in a *tonga*. She ran after the *tonga* for about a mile, wrestled the camera and smashed it."

## P R Avasthi and Mother

"In December 1914, P R Avasthi went with me to Shirdi. He had received *guru* mantra from a woman Saint in his younger days, and did not know if she was alive. H S Dixit was his friend and he wanted him to go to Baba for *darshan*. Avasthi thought that it would be *guru droha* (faithlessness towards his guru). When he came to know of my association with the Master, he spoke of the state of his mind. I told him that Baba was a super guru and was one with god. He agreed to come with me provided I took the responsibility. Baba asked me who this person was. Avasthi got very excited.

"The next day Mother tied some mogra flowers together and handing them over to me, said, "Take this to the Master, and ask him to unravel it." Baba smelt the flowers and returned them with the message that she should do it.

"In the meantime Avasthi had a brain wave. He made a *Pindam* (small rice ball) out of the *naivedya*, this was not known to us. He decided that if Baba accepted it, he would conclude that his guru was no more, and taking Baba as his Guru would not be *guru droha*.

"I went with him to the Masjid with the *naivedya*, the *pindam* in his hand was under the plate. Baba said, "Give it to me." He took the *pinda,* smelt it and said, "It has reached its place." We returned to Mother's residence and the moment he stepped at the door, Avasthi rushed to Mother and fell at her feet. He was singing spontaneously, for about half an hour, unconscious of his surroundings. The Mother was in a trance. Later, he told me that in place of Mother he had seen his first Guru."

## Pain does not hinder her service to the Master
"In 1914, I was doubtful about my ability to attend the *Gurupurnima* function. The food was to be cooked in Mother's house. But she said that if I was not there, it better be cooked elsewhere. On *Gurupurnima* day she got an extra quota from Baba's *bhiksha*, and she came to know that I was coming, and the cooking started.

"They wanted a stone to pound the spices. The step leading to the house was considered good, and Mother and I moved it with some difficulty. Just as it was in front of the door frame, Purandhare (a devotee) came up and wanted to help. The stone turned and it might have crushed my hand but Mother pulled it towards herself and the index finger of her right hand was crushed into two. She soaked a rag in oil and wrapped the bleeding finger, and went on to help in the cooking.

38

"Only after everything was over, she called me and said that she was feeling the pain and would like to go to the jungle and cry. We went there and for about half an hour she cried. Then we came back and did our normal work. What control over the body and indifference to pleasure and pain in the service of the Master."

## Mother passes away

I quote, "In my last letter I remember having mentioned the incident of Baba coming from the Lendi Baugh. Mai having washed the floor of the Masjid was in a trance. Baba stroked her back and asked her not to worry.

"Two months after this incident, Mother passed away. I went to Shirdi and not knowing where I should stay, I went straight to the Masjid. Baba told me to go to Dixit *wada* and stay there. Shama and many others offered me condolences.

"Baba called us and asked us about the conversation. The Master said, 'What do these fools know? She was your mother and mine. She wanted to be freed from her karma and I gave her my assurance. One night she came to me and said that she could not wait anymore and got in here...' (Baba lifted up his *kafni*, and pointed to his heart). 'You will see her here when you desire.' My divine mother is merged in the master. Let people in their own way imagine what they will. I cannot forget what I owe to her." Rege then concludes his letter by saying, "Shri Mhalsapathy and Shri H S Dixit had great reverence for her and I feel I am in good company."

Radha Krishna Mai through her dedication and hard work made Baba's *Sansthan* into what it is today. Now the devotees of Shri Sai Baba can behold the splendour of the *palki* and *rath* procession, along with the different *lalkari* by the *chopdars*.

Ref: *Rege had written this letter on 3rd September, 1968 to Sridhar answering his queries about Radha Krishna Mai*

## Some little known facts about Mai

B V Dev writes a glowing account of Radha Krishna Mai. He says that Radha Krishna Mai came to Shirdi from Pandharpur along with Nana Sahib Chandokar in 1905. Her name was Sundrabai Ksheersagar, she was a child widow and when she came to Shirdi she was about 25 years old. She passed away at the young age of 35 years.

Mai was totally devoted to Baba, and she wanted Baba to have all the grandeur of Vitthal. The congregational worship of Baba was started by her, along with all the grandeur of the umbrella, *chowri* (whisk), etc. When Baba slept in the *Chavdi*, the *lalkari* (loud salutations to Baba) of the *chopdars* (uniformed men giving the *lalkari*), the *bhajans* along with musical instruments, the horse, the *Taj* and flags were due to Mai's effort.

Mai was responsible for the congregational worship. She also saw that *Sej arati* (night *arati*) and *Kakad arati* (early morning *arati*) were performed daily and on time. Although, she was at Shirdi for about 8 years, she accomplished what a man would not be able to do even in 25 years. Through her *seva* and perseverance, she gave shape to the present *Sansthan*. Day in and day out she worked, doing whatever Baba needed, and also made the other devotees do the same. She was respected a lot and no one dared to disobey her.

Mai was never without a *ghungat* (face covered by the rear end of the sari) in front of Baba, nor did she ever ascend the steps of the Dwaraka Mai in Baba's presence. This was a mark of respect. She felt that Baba was her husband in her previous life. Shama said that Baba once told him, "Mai was close to me in my previous life. But I had no bodily contact with her." Mai had a small idol of Krishna with her, at all times. Even when she went to the bathroom, the idol went with her. So she was called Radha Krishna Mai.

With her effort, Baba's fakiri was turned into a *rajya yog* (royal appearance). Daily she sent *Govind paan vida* for Baba. *Govind* is the shape of the *vida*, the ingredients are placed on the *paan*, and the shape is conical, so it's easy to put in the mouth and chew, *paan* is beetle nut leaf, *vida* is the final shape given to it.

Dr Gavankar states that Baba loved *paan*, and chewed it at all times. In fact, he chewed a lot of *paan*. Kondaji Lalbhai Sheak, a Muslim devotee residing at Riktshi, *talluqa* Shevgaon in Ahmednagar district, provided Baba with hundreds of *paan vidas*. Baba would often throw a *vida* on some devotee, and make him eat it. Simultaneously Baba also ate a *vida*, and drank some water after that.

After the arrival of Radha Krishna Mai, she provided *paan vida* for Baba. She sent *tambul,* (pounded *paan vida*) to Baba after his lunch. Baba after having it drank water. This ritual is still being carried on by the *Sansthan.*

## Mai lights the lantern

When Baba went to the *Chavdi* on alternate days, she had a ritual of lighting the lantern in the Dwaraka Mai. In the evening after having a bath, she wore a snow white sari, covered her face, and went to the Dwaraka Mai. There she lit a lantern that had five wicks and placed it on the step leading into the sanctum sanctorum. The white sari she wore was treasured by her as it was bought and given to her by Baba. Every day Baba sent food from his *bhiksha* (one *roti*, and some vegetable dish as *prasad*) on this she survived.

Ref: *Sai Leela Chaitra, Vaishak, Jyeshth Shake 1852. Ank 1, 2 and 3. Year 14 (1938)*

Leela 31: ## Baba hai Dattache aayhe
### (Baba is Lord Dattatreya)

Once the eldest son of Moreshwar Pradan was extremely sick. At that time a Telenge gentleman named Shastri Bua was staying with them. He was devoted to Lord Dattatreya, and did not approve of the families devotion to Baba. He was very concerned about the sick child, so he asked Pradhan to give up his devotion towards Baba and pray to Lord Datta for the recovery of the child's health. Pradhan told him that Baba was none other than Lord Datta.

So Shastri Bua proposed a test. He said, "If within five minutes the child drinks a glass of milk, then I will believe that Baba is Datta. And if by tomorrow the child starts recovering, I will go to Shirdi for Baba's *darshan* and give Rs 125 as *dakshind*", and so it came to pass.

The child within few minutes asked for milk, which he drank happily. The next day, he started recovering. When the child had recovered completely, Shastri Bua went to Shirdi as per his vow and gave Baba Rs 125 as *dakshina*. That evening Baba asked Shastri Bua to give him five rupees as *dakshina*. Shama who was there, said, "Baba, just this morning the man gave you Rs 125. Why are you asking him to give you five rupees?" Baba said, "The Rs 125 he gave me this morning were offered to his Datta, where did I get them?" Shastri Bua was astonished to hear this. He respectfully placed five rupees in Baba's hand.          Ref: *Sai Leela Aashad Shake 1845. Ank 5. Year 1*

*Leela 32:*                 # Shantaram, Balwant Nachne and the tiger

On 31-3-1915, Nachne and a colleague of his, named Shantaram M Panse, were returning home. They had just completed their official assignment. The route was through a dense forest. The only mode of transportation was by bullock cart. It was rather late at night when they reached the Ranset pass. This forest was known to be populated by tigers.

By then it was quite dark. The bullock cart started rolling backwards. They wondered what was causing the bulls to move back. They could not discern any reason at first. Then they noticed that the road ahead was broken on one side and there were boulders that had dislodged and fallen on the other side. If the cart swerved a little, then all of them including the bulls and the cart would have fallen into the deep ravine below.

Just then Panse pointed his finger in front of him. Nachne looked straight and into the glinting eyes of a tiger. The tiger had jumped from the rocks on the other side. If the bulls in terror swerved a little they would have fallen to their death, whereas if they got down and prevented the cart from rolling back, the tiger would have made a meal of them.

Nonetheless Panse, judging the gravity of the situation, wanted to get down and place a stone or rock behind the wheels. This would prevent the cart from rolling backwards. He handed the reins over to Nachne and got down from the other side.

Nachne all of a sudden started shouting at the top of his voice, "Hail Sai Baba. Baba, run and come to our aid." Panse also joined in. This frightened the tiger, and it slunk away. Nachne's faith in Baba as his saviour made him call out to Baba and a danger was averted.

The *rinanubandhic* ties between Baba, and Nachne and his family were deep and unfathomable. Baba looked after their health, prosperity and spiritual well being. On one of Nachne's visits to Shirdi, Baba gave him these small silver *padukas*.

Nachne carried this precious gift home and enshrined it in his prayer room. He accorded the *padukas* the same reverence, which he wholeheartedly gave to Baba. This tradition is still followed by his descendants who live in Thane, and daily worship the *padukas*.

Ref: *Sai Leela Aashad Shake 1845. Ank 5. Year 1*

## Leela 33: **Vishnupanth Pithale makes a pilgrimage to Shirdi**

Vishnupanth Pithale and his family lived in Vile Parle, a suburb of Bombay. He worked as a *thalathi*, and had a keen desire to visit Shirdi and have Baba's *darshan*. In 1917, he visited Shirdi for the first time Carefully he made all the preparations. He roamed the fruit markets, so he could get the choicest, unripe mangoes. Finally he found a fruit vendor, who had delectable mangoes. Making sure that the mangoes were unblemished and unripe, he bought a basket. Then he set out for Shirdi, thinking that 'if I get ripe mangoes, they will spoil by the time I reach Shirdi. Whereas these unripe mangoes will ripen there.'

He reached Kopergaon, and proceeded thence to Shirdi. Baba was seated with his devotees in the Dwaraka Mai. Suddenly the Dwaraka Mai was filled with the aroma of mangoes. The devotees looked at each other wondering where the mangoes were kept. As Baba said nothing they just waited.

## Vishnupanth offers Baba ripe delectable mangoes

Vishnupanth in the mean time reached Shirdi. He kept his luggage and the mangoes in the room and went for *dhule darshan* (*dhule* means dust and *darshan* is homage). The pilgrim goes right away for *darshan* without having a bath, and the dust from the journey is still on him. Baba welcomed him, saying, "What have you brought for me? Where are the mangoes?" Vishnupanth was abashed, and said, "Baba, the mangoes are in the room as they are unripe." Baba replied, "Go fetch them, can't you smell them." Vishnupanth went to the room, and brought the basket and placed it before Baba. Upon opening it he was surprised that the mangoes had ripened perfectly and was ready to eat.

## Vishnupanth gives Baba Rs 15 as dakshina

Happily Vishnupanth, stayed at Shirdi for three days. He made sure that he had 15 rupees kept away for his return journey. On the day of his departure, he bought a photograph of Baba. He took it to the Dwaraka Mai hoping that Baba would bless it with his touch. Baba called him, saying, "Bhau, give me Rs 15/- as *dakshina*." Vishnupanth, at once emptied his pocket and gave the 15 rupees. Baba then, asked him for the photograph. Vishnupanth handed him the photograph. Baba took the photograph and hugged it for a moment.

Vishnupanth was extremely happy but was in a quandary, as he had no money for his return journey. Finally, he decided to walk to Kopergaon as he did not have money to hire a *tonga*. He walked about half a mile or so when a *tonga* drew up and stopped near him. The driver said, "What are you doing, walking in the heat of the day? You do not look like a villager?" Vishnupanth replied, "I am a *thalathi*, and I am going to the next village." Vishnupanth did not want to tell him that he did not have money, as Baba had taken all of it. The *tonga* driver laughed and said, "Come and have a seat, I will take you to Kopergaon." At the station he alighted from the *tonga*, and collected his luggage. He looked up to thank the driver, but the driver and the *tonga* had disappeared.

He went into the station and looked around hoping, he would find some acquaintance. But there was no one around to borrow the money from. Finally, the train pulled in and he decided to travel ticketless and bear the consequences. At the next station the ticket collector entered his compartment, and looking at him, he said, "Namaskar, Pithale Sahib." Vishnupanth, however, did not recognise him. He feared that since the ticket collector had recognised him, he would surely ask him for his ticket. It would cause a great deal of embarrassment. But no such thing happened and he reached Bombay without any problem.

The very next day a huge automobile pulled up in front of his doorstep. A well-dressed gentleman came to his home and enquired, "Are you *thalathi*, Vishnupanth Pithale?" Vishnupanth was bewildered and thought, 'I must be in trouble now, why is he asking if I am a *thalathi*?' The gentleman said, "I am Mr Tata. I am in the process of buying a land at Sahara (the present airport). I have a huge staff on my payroll. But they can't transcribe the Marathi papers into English a vice versa. I heard that you are a capable *thalathi* and bilingual." Vishnupanth was aghast at what he heard, and nodded his head. Then the gentleman continued, "As a *thalathi* you earn only Rs 35/- a month. If you agree to work for me I will pay you Rs 150/- per month." Quickly Vishnupanth said, "I will do the transcription for you, but give me two days to think about working for you." Tata said, "All right?" And he drove away.

Vishnupanth was in turmoil now. 'What if I give up my government job with pension benefits, and this man does not keep his word? What if he dismisses me after his work is done?' he thought. He spent a restless night. Suddenly it dawned on him that Baba had emptied his pocket of Rs 15/- and is now returning it tenfold. Two days later Tata's secretary came to his home with the 'appointment letter' and details of the job benefits. Vishnupanth bowed to the photograph that Baba had hugged and signed on the dotted line.

So Baba gave him tenfold of the Rs 15/- he took as *dakshina*.

Ref: *As narrated by his grandson, Manohar Pithale*

## His descendants

Amol and Shraddha Pithale are physicians practicing medicine in Mumbai. They spend their spare time doing social service. The most valuable service that they render is giving first aid and treating the myriad of devotees who walk, with the *palki* from Mumbai to Shirdi prior to Ram Navami. This service is free for the devotees.

In fact, this trend of giving first aid to the devotees was started by them a few years ago.

## *Leela 34:* **The atheist 'Keshev R Pradhan'**

Inscrutable are the mystic ways of Baba, for when he showers his grace, the impossible and unimaginable is possible. Baba rarely left Shirdi physically, except to go to Rahatha, Nigoj and occasionally to Rui. In this *leela*, he goes to Ukrool village. This village is near Bhivpuri road.

Keshev R Pradhan was a hard core atheist, whereas his dearest friend was an ardent devotee of Baba. Pradhan worked for a bill collection agency run by a Parsi gentleman in Mumbai. His job entailed him to go to Manmad, Nasik and Kopergaon for bill collections. His friend who frequently visited Shirdi urged him to go to Shirdi either during an official tour or to accompany him. But all his requests fell on deaf ears.

After much cajoling and even coercion, Pradhan finally agreed to accompany his friend. Before he made the trip, he told his friend emphatically and clearly that he wouldn't step into the Masjid. After he was quite sure that his friend had agreed, only then did he accompany him.

## Pradhan attends an arati in Dwaraka Mai

Upon reaching Shirdi they rented a room and stayed there. Soon it was time for the noon *arati,* and his friend went to the Dwaraka Mai leaving Pradhan in the room. At twelve o' clock the *arati* started, and the peals of bells ringing filled the air, and charged the atmosphere with spiritual energy. The sounds of the bells ringing reached Pradhan's room. He got restless and soon it turned into a hypnotic spell. He stood up and swayed to their beats. Before he realised, he was walking in that direction. He entered the Dwaraka Mai and stood amongst the rest of the devotees.

When the *arati* was over, the devotees went for Baba's *darshan* one by one. Pradhan, however, sat in a corner and looked at Baba with intense concentration. Try as he may, he could not take his eyes off Baba's divine form. He sat there and gazed at Baba enchantedly.

## Pradhan empties his pocket for dakshina

Soon the Dwaraka Mai was empty, and Baba beckoned him over with a wave. Still in a daze he went and sat in front of Baba. With a smile Baba put out his hand and asked for *dakshina*. Pradhan thrust his hand in to his pocket and handed over Rs 2,500/- (the entire sum he had collected for the agency). Then in the same dazed state he returned to his room. When he came to his normal state he was mortified at what he had done. Thinking about the money he realised he did not have enough money to return home let alone repay his employer.

Nonetheless he started for Kopergaon by *tonga*. As he did not have any money with him he took off his gold ring and gave it to the *tonga* driver. Pradhan requested him to sell the ring and take the fare from it. Suddenly a well-dressed gentleman appeared on the scene and paid the *tonga* driver. He again proceeded to buy a ticket to Bombay and efficiently made all arrangements for a comfortable journey. He then seated Pradhan in the train and disappeared in the crowd. Pradhan was speechless and wondered at the kindness of the gentleman.

## The leela of the dakshina given to Baba unfolds

Pradhan reached home but was in a turmoil about the repayment of the money to his employer. He wasn't affluent. He wondered how he would repay it, and what explanation he would give. So he called in sick. Pradhan sent word to his employer that he may be absent for a long time due to illness. The employer granted him the leave, and told him to return only after he had fully recovered. He also told him not to worry as he had received twice the amount of money that was due. Pradhan was astounded to hear this, and it dawned on him that the kind gentleman who helped him and the recovery of the payments were Baba's *leelas*. From that time onwards the atheist turned into an ardent devotee.

## Baba goes to stay at Bhivpuri

The above event had such a profound effect on him that he started visiting Shirdi as often as he could. After *darshan* he would request Baba to come to Ukrool (Bhivpuri). This he did on each and every visit. In 1916 he visited Shirdi and requested Baba to come to his home. Baba picked up one of his bass replicas given to him by a devotee and handing it to Pradhan said, "Go back to Bhivpuri. Erect a temple and place this replica of me in it. Start all the functions there and don't come here again, for that is your Shirdi."

Pradhan brought the bass replica to Bhivpuri but did not follow Baba's orders. When he visited Shirdi again, Baba said, "When I have come to your house why do you come here? Bhivpuri is your Shirdi now." After a few days he erected a small temple and installed the bass replica. There he performed *pujas* daily, and all the festivals were celebrated.

The temple is built adjacent to his house. It is serene and beautiful. It has abundant trees and is surrounded by luscious greenery. In front of the temple and to the left is a huge and ancient *peepul* tree, and next to it is a banyan tree.

Once at midnight Pradhan heard the temple door open. He and his family went to see who it was! What they saw left them spellbound. They saw Baba enter the temple and close the door behind him. At 3 a.m. the door opened again and Baba left. Pradhan narrated this wonderful experience to all his friends and relatives, who also came to behold this wonderful event.

Pradhan passed away in 1939. But before this he left the management of the temple to his sons and son-in-law, A V Gupta, an ardent devotee of Baba. The temple soon became famous in the neighbouring villages, in Bombay and other places. As devotees flocked there, an expansion plan was undertaken. This plan was halted for a while due to lack of funds. So a devotee named Narayan Purohit started doing a *parayan* of the *Satcharita* to find a solution. On the fourth day Baba appeared in his dream and said, "Where is my *dhuni*? There is no *dhuni* here, then how can it be Shirdi?" When Baba orders something, he also finds a solution. The *dhuni* was lit by Dev Baba and the total expenses were borne by Kumar Sen Samrath.

This is a 'must visit' temple.

## Leela 35: Dev Baba alias Ananth Prabhu Walvalkar

❝The delivery will be without any problems as one of my sons will be born to her," said Baba. This was Baba's promise to Dabolkar, when he visited Shirdi. Dabolkar had gone there to seek Baba's help as his daughter was behaving strangely during her pregnancy. Thus, Dev Baba was born with Baba's blessings on the 13th of April, 1918.

His life story is given in the book called *Baba's Rinanubandh*. Dev Baba exhibited his divinity from a very  young age. Baba blessed him with many *sidhis* that he used very wisely. He was extremely good at predicting events that were to occur in peoples lives, thus he was instrumental in averting many calamities that people might have had to face. Besides, he was kind and loved to help the sick and the infirm.

One of his qualities was to take upon himself the illnesses of other people.  Whenever he did this, he became very sick. He also gave relief to many pregnant ladies whenever they had complications during pregnancy. At that time Dev Baba's body would look like that of a pregnant female. This 'taking of the illness on himself' made him go through excruciating pain, bloating and swelling of the feet.

Often he suffered labour pains for hours on end, but the lady concerned had an easy delivery. Invariably after the delivery Dev Baba had to rest for a day or two.

Ref: *Dev Babachaya chhayeth by Shankar Rajjan Apte, Mumbai*

## Leela 36: Dattatreya Deshpande Nimonkar

His ancestors hailed from Nimongaon, so they were called 'the Nimonkars'. They were 'Deshpandes' by caste. Nimongaon is about 20 miles away from Shirdi. His grandfather, Nana Sahib Nimonkar, was Madhavrao Deshpande's (Shama's) paternal uncle. Shama and his ancestors also hailed from Nimongaon. When Shama was 2 years old they moved to Shirdi. Balwantrao (Shama's father) brought Nana Sahib to have Baba's *darshan*, after that Nana stayed on and made Shirdi his home.

Dattatreya, Nana Sahib's nephew, was born in December of 1917. That December, plague was playing havoc in Poona, so Somnath (Nana Sahib's son) decided to go to Nimongaon along with his 2-year-old son, called Gopalrao. On the way they stopped at Shirdi for Baba's *darshan*. When they were leaving Baba gave them *udi* and said, "*Pora la jiv lav*" (save the child). Somnath thought that Baba had blessed his child Gopalrao, so he gave him some *udi*.

They reached Nimongaon and found Dattatreya at death's door. The child, only 12 days old, was blue and cold, and was gasping for air. It was then that Somnath realised that Baba had given him *udi* to save Dattatreya's life. Frantically he searched for the *udi*. But it was lost during the journey. Somnath took the child and sent a fervent prayer to Baba to save the child. Baba came to his aid and after 15 minutes, the body temperature returned to normal, the breathing grew steady and the baby's condition improved. The child was thus named Datta (that is 'God's gift').

Datta was a bright lad and studied up to 7th standard in Marathi medium school. He participated in all the activities of the village, and as his civic duty he voted during the elections. He owned vast acres of land, and he made a living by farming.

He lives with his extended family in Nimongaon.

Ref: *As narrated by Datta himself*

## Leela 37: Chottu Bhaya Parulkar receives a portrait and padukas of Baba

Chottu Bhaya was an ardent devotee of Baba. Baba loved him immensely. An artist by the name M Radhakrishna Rao of Bombay made a sketch portrait of Baba on 7-6-1914. He was completely enamoured of Baba's luminous *roopa* (form). Dixit, Kaka Mahajani and every devotee who saw the portrait liked it a lot. The devotees knew that Baba would be extremely angry upon seeing it. They decided to keep it in the Dwaraka Mai and covered it with a white cloth.

Fervently they hoped that Baba would be in a good mood, so they could show it to him. The noon *arati* was peaceful, and Baba didn't get angry at any point. After the *arati,* Baba was smiling so Shama said, "*Deva,* an artist has made your sketch. We would like you to see it." Even before he could finish speaking, Baba roared, "Where is the portrait? Bring it before me. Why are you making my portrait? Bring it at once!"

The devotees meekly brought the portrait and placed it before Baba. Rolling his eyes, he picked up his *satka* (Baton) and lunged towards the portrait, and was about to strike it. But suddenly he became calm. Shama said, "*Deva,* what is to be done with the portrait?" The devotees were standing transfixed and waiting. Baba looked in all four directions, and at every devotee that was present there. Chottu Bhaya was standing next to Baba. Baba turned towards him and said softly, "Take this portrait with you, and everything of yours will become gold." The drawing is 2½ by 3½ inches in dimensions. Chottu Bhaya took the portrait home and venerated it.

## Baba gave Chottu Bhaya padukas

On another occasion, a devotee from Poona gave Baba *padukas*. That day Baba went to Lendi Baugh wearing the *padukas*, which was rather unusual. Returning from Lendi Baugh, he took off the *padukas*, washed his feet and went into the sanctum sanctorum. Then he gave Chottu Bhaya the *padukas*.

The portrait and the *padukas* are still with the descendants. At their home in Harda, this portrait and *padukas* are being worshipped daily.

*Leela 38:*  # The Locket

Tatya Sahib Nulkar took *samadhi* (died) in 1911 in Shirdi. He was only 48 years old at that time. His mother (Janki Bai) had made a locket, on one side it had Baba's image and facing Baba was Tatya's image. She sent it by mail to Shirdi, care of Shama, hoping that Baba would bless it with his touch. The parcel arrived at the Dwaraka Mai, and Shama received it. There was also a letter in it in Marathi.

Shama after receiving the parcel, wrote this letter to the mother. The letter read:

Shirdi, Date 20-12-1912

Humble Salutations,

Yesterday, i.e., on Thursday the 19th, at the time of *arati*, the postman delivered to Sai Maharaj the locket parcel sent by you. Sai Maharaj took it and moving the box round his face, kissed it. He then said to me, "There are two persons in this", and handed over the parcel to me. On opening the parcel I found a locket with the photographs of Baba and Tatya and the letter. I read the letter to Sai Maharaj and handed over the locket to him. He held the locket in his hand for about 15 to 20 minutes and showed it to almost every one that came for the *arati*. Baba then said,

"This person took me away with him." The exact words said by Sai Maharaj have been written down and sent to you. The locket has been handed over to me for safe custody.

My respects to you.

Sai Das
Madhavrao Deshpande

This incident gives just a glimpse of the love and regard Baba had for Tatya Sahib. Baba equates Tatya Sahib with himself, and vouches his advanced spiritual development. Baba also acknowledges the fact that Tatya Sahib has merged with him.

Baba gave Tatya Sahib many things, like coins of various denominations, his *kafni*, etc. These were materialistic things, but spiritually he gave him *sadgati*.

Ref: *Tatya Sahib's grandson, Raghunath V Nulkar, provided the letter and information to Lt. Col. M B Nimbalkar, who published an article in the Sai Leela Magazine May-June 1991*

## Leela 39:   Seetadevi Ramchandra Tarkhad

It is an impossible task to write about this devotee, but I will try my best to give you some idea of the love and regard Baba had for her.

Her maiden name was Krishnabai Kusumbarkar. She was affluent, cultured and educated. Her husband was also very affluent, he was an expert in textiles and was the secretary of Khatau Mills. After her marriage to Ramchandra A Tarkhad, she had all the comforts life could offer. But all this didn't make her happy as she had severe migraine. There were a slew of doctors on both sides of her family and she was treated by all of them. But there was no relief. Soon she started having 'cluster headaches'. The headaches became more frequent and intense.

## Seetadevi visits Pir Maulana Sahib

There was a constant look of pain and suffering on her face. One day her maid suggested that she should visit Pir Maulana Sahib who was famous for treating and curing many ailments. At that point of time she was willing to do anything to get some relief from the terrible throbbing and pounding in her head.

Seetadevi confided in her son, Jyotindra, who was very enterprising, and they devised a plan. *Pir* Maulana had a *dargah* near Bandra Masjid. In those days it was almost impossible for a Hindu lady to go to a Muslim *pir*, hence the elaborate plan. Jyotindra got a *hijab* for his mother (dress worn by conservative Muslims which covers the whole body) and took her by car to the *dargah*.

## The rinanubandhic ties start unfolding

The *pir,* however, could not help her, for he said, "I cannot help you, but my brother at Shirdi, Sai Baba, surely can. Go to him." Thus the *rinanubandhic* ties started unfolding. Again Jyotindra came to her rescue, he asked the people at the Iranian restaurant about Shirdi. He gathered all the information that he possibly could get. Now all that remained was to make the pilgrimage to Shirdi. This was a formidable task, as his father was a *Prathna Samajist* (who did not believe in idol worship), let alone going to sadhus or babas. Finally he got permission, but there were other questions about the location of Shirdi, and about their stay there. Jyotindra found all the necessary information, as best as he could.

One Friday evening they made the 'life transforming' journey, and they reached Shirdi on Saturday in the morning. After having a bath, Seetadevi and Jyotindra went to the Dwaraka Mai. Baba was sitting in his usual place facing *dhuni Ma*.

Mrs Tarkhad, bent and touched Baba's feet, and they looked at each other. The eyes locked, it was an intense look, and Baba looked into her very soul. This was *dhrusti path* (transference of divine energy).

Baba said, "Mother, you have come? My brother at Bandra sent you to me, isn't it so? Mother come and sit here. You have extreme pain in your head. Right?" While he was thus speaking Baba put the palm of his hand into a dish containing *udi*. Swiftly he took his *udi-*

*laden* hand and hit Seetadevi with a great deal of force on her forehead. Simultaneously he held her head in his grip. While he did this, he said, "आये आतापासून आपल्या अंतापर्यंत हे तुझे डोके कधीच दुखणार नाही घ्याची पीड आता संपली।।"

"Ayi, from now on till the end of your life, your head will never ever hurt again. Your suffering has now come to an end." All this time Seetadevi had not spoken a word. Indeed the tormenting pain left her. The look of anguish and suffering also faded away and her face had a blissful and calm look.

Here two things happened, first Baba gave her a long intense look, which was *dhrusti path*. The second thing which happened was that he hit her forehead and squeezed the pain out of her head. This was *shakti path*. Seetadevi turned to Jyotindra and asked him to touch Baba's feet.

Baba loved Seetadevi, and had great respect for her. Although she was rather young, Baba called her 'Ayi' and meant it. Baba saw the total innocence of this gentle lady as she knew no disgust or repulsion towards a mongrel (dog) or a mud-splattered pig. In Chapter 9 of *Shri Sai Satcharita,* the story of her feeding a hungry dog and then a filthy pig is given.

It is hard to find adjectives for this lady, because one runs out of them, and nor do they convey the essence of her nature. One just has to feel and perceive it.

## Jyotindra meets a fakir

Jyotindra came to Shirdi at a very young age. The wonderful *leela* of his meeting Baba prior to his visit is given below.

It was his daily routine to have lunch at an Iranian restaurant, near Metro Cinema. One day he had lunch at the restaurant and was crossing the road to return to St. Xavier's School, when he was accosted by a fakir. The fakir wore a white robe and he begged him for alms. Jyotindra, immediately put his hand in his pocket and gave him a paisa, and was about to leave, but the fakir stopped him and told him that the one paisa coin was of the year 1894. A paisa is a copper coin with a hole in the centre. One paisa is a large amount to be given in charity, and that too, by a student. Jyotindra reassured him that it was all right as he got 4 *annas* daily as pocket money. The fakir laughed and said, "*Allah bhalla karega*" (Allah will do good), and went away.

Some time later, he went with his mother to Shirdi, seeking a cure for her headaches. His mother asked him to bow at Baba's feet. Then Baba said, "Bhau, didn't you recognise me?" Jyotindra had not recognised him. Then Baba said, "*Arre*, look directly at me, and try to remember." As Jyotindra looked at Baba, Baba looked into his eyes and their gaze locked with intensity, and he was changed forever. He racked his brains trying to remember, when Baba put his hand in his pocket and took out the copper coin.

The rest as they say was history.   Ref: *Shri Sai Swanubhav Tarkhadache*


*Leela 40:*     # Baba saves Jyotindra's life in a 'cloud burst'

When you enter Shirdi from Kopergaon, you cross a small bridge that spans a small rivulet. Now it's known as Lakshmi Nagar. This rivulet is dry most of the year, but in the monsoons it is filled with water. In those days there was no proper sanitation, or toilet facilities. The villagers and devotees used the place as a toilet. They went there before dawn as the traffic was light on the road above.

On one occasion, Jyotindra was in Shirdi during the monsoons. It was his habit to go to the rivulet very early, then go to his room, have a bath and then attend *Kakad arati*. It was drizzling, and as he went out, he took an umbrella and a flash light. A while later, he heard a man shouting, he was on the other bank of the stream, "*Londha alare ala pala*" (A torrent of water is headed this way. Now run for safety.)

## Baba melo mala wachava
Jyotindra did not understand the meaning of *londha*, as he did know the colloquial dialect. However, he heard the urgency in his tone and

his warning to run to safety. He stood up, and flashed the light to see what was happening. What he saw frightened him, a huge wall of black-coloured water was descending upon him. It was death staring at him, for he would surely drown. He closed his eyes and beseeched Baba to save him from a watery grave. He said, "बाबा मेलो मला वाचवा ॥"

"*Baba melo mala wachava*" (Baba, I am going to die, save me.) After some time he realised he was alive, and not washed away. He opened his eyes to find that the water had disappeared and he was standing on a dry land. Whereas on either side the water was raging. Along with its fury many dead goats, snakes and branches of trees flowed by. While this was happening, he was continuously chanting Baba's name.

He knew that only Baba's grace has saved him, so mentally he thanked Baba. Jyotindra waited for the water to recede and when it was about knee high he slowly waded through it and came to his room.

Upon reaching his room he told his mother all that had happened. His mother heard what he had to say with disbelief, but she knew who his saviour was. She told him to go immediately and thank Baba. Jyotindra with *puja* materials and a heart bursting with gratitude went to the Dwaraka Mai. He had hardly climbed the steps leading to the sanctum sanctorum, when Baba said, "*Arre* Bhau, today before dawn, why were you yelling my name for help? Are you frightened of death?" Jyotindra held Baba's feet tightly and said, "Baba, you are a *antaryami* (one who resides in your heart and knows every thing) and for an ordinary man like me, death is frightening. In a situation like this, you are my only refuge, so I shouted for help." Baba replied, "भाऊ उठ, अरे वेड्या मी तुला शिर्डीला जे ओढून आणतो ते काय अरे मरण्यासाठी ? भाऊ आपण असे सहजासहजी नाही मरायचो आपल्याला अजून खुप कार्य करायचे आहे ॥"

"Bhau, get up. *Arre*, do I pull you to Shirdi so you can die? You are not going to die so easily. You still have a lot of work to do.".

Ref: *Shri Sai Swanubhav Tarakhadache*

## Leela 41: Baba comes in the form of a photograph to stay in the Tarkhad home

In *Shri Sai Satcharita* Chapter 9, the story of Ramchandra Tarkhad and his son Jyotindra is given. How Jyotindra extracted a promise from his father to worship Baba's photograph in the sandalwood shrine daily. Jyotindra followed this routine rather strictly. He got up every day at 5 a.m., had a bath, and then did *puja*. He applied sandalwood paste to Baba's photograph. Then lighted incense and offered *naivedya* of sugar candy. Thus he was reluctant to accompany his mother to Shirdi, as he did not want a break in this routine.

Ramchandra assured him again and again that he would perform *puja* daily and offer *naivedya* to Baba, and then have his lunch. Only after Jyotindra was fully convinced of his father's promise did he accompany his mother. But one day his father forgot to offer *naivedya*. There at Shirdi, Baba said, "What to do O! Mother? Today as every day I went to your home in Bandra, but there was no rice, no gruel, nothing to eat or drink. And hungry I have to return." (*Ovi* 107)

### How Baba came to the Tarkhad House in the form of a photograph?

In *Shri Sai Satcharita* Chapter 40, Baba goes to Dabolkar's home in the form of a bass relief. In this *leela* Baba goes to the Tarkhad house in the form of a photograph. One day early in the morning, Jyotindra and his father had an identical dream. They both saw a beautiful sandalwood *devera* (shrine) and Baba sitting in it. They immediately got up and made a sketch of it. When they met for breakfast, they spoke of their dream. They were astonished to find that their dream was identical, and the sketch that each had drawn was same.

They decided to have such a *devera* as soon as possible. They set out and bought a lot of sandalwood. Then brought a carpenter and showed him the sketches, and commissioned him to make the shrine. Their residence at Bandra had a small terrace, and there the carving of the shrine started.

It took about a year to complete it. After completion, the *devera* stood nine feet tall, and two feet five inches by two feet five inches in length and breadth. So it was a masterpiece. Now they wanted a beautiful photograph of Baba. They knew that Baba did not allow himself to be photographed, so what was to be done?

One Friday evening, father and son were strolling in Chor Bazar, when a shopkeeper started gesticulating at them to come to his shop. Then the shopkeeper ran after them and said he had a packet for them. Jyotindra and his father entered the shop rather sceptically.

Then the wonderful *leela* started unfolding. They questioned the shopkeeper about the parcel. The shopkeeper said, "A few days ago, a saintly looking, elderly gentleman came to my shop. He said, 'On Friday a Hindu father and his son will pass this way. You can easily recognise them as the father will have on a hat, and the son will have a black Gandhi cap.' He then handed me this packet and also gave me Rs 50/- as service charges. Please accept this packet." They still were sceptical so they asked the shopkeeper to open it. What they saw left them speechless. It was a beautiful photograph of Baba sitting on the stone.

They thanked him and offered him some money for the trouble he had taken; but he refused to accept the money. Jyotindra and his father returned home. They placed the photograph in the *devera*, and it fit perfectly.

On there next visit to Shirdi they went to the Dwaraka Mai. At that time a local devotee was trying to get a photograph of Baba. When Baba said, "अरे फोटो फोटो काय करतोस माझ्या भाऊंच्या घरी जाऊन पहा मी तिथे जिवंत बसलेला आहे ।।"

"Arre photo photo kay kartos, maje bhaucha ghari jaun paha me jeevanth baslela aahye." (Roughly translated – Go to my Bhau's house, and see. I am alive and sitting there.) Jyotindra got up at once and held his feet. Mentally he prayed for only one boon and that was to never ever forget Baba.        Ref: *Shri Sai Swanubhav Tarkhadache*

*Leela 42:*        # Baba gives life to Malanbai

❝The moment you put your foot on the soil of Shirdi your sufferings would end. The Fakir of this place is very kind. He will eradicate your disease and pain," said Baba to Bhimaji patil of Narayangaon (*Shri Sai Satcharita* Chapter 13, *Ovi* 72 and 74). Bhimaji was suffering from pulmonary tuberculosis. Though myriads of remedies and treatments were considered, they miserably failed. So along with Nana he came to Shirdi.

It was Baba's word and it had to be followed accurately, and a cure was inevitable. Here is another *leela* about pulmonary tuberculosis.

Malanbai was the daughter of Damodar Ranganath Joshi Degaonkar. She was extremely sick with pulmonary tuberculosis. It started with a fever that was relentless, and continued for months. Finally, it affected her lungs. She became emaciated, and could neither sit up nor turn to her side. Various doctors and *vaids* (alternative medical professionals) treated her, but of no avail. She was tired of taking the medicines, so as a last resort her father started giving her Baba's *udi*, simultaneously he continued the medications. She incessantly asked her father to take her to Shirdi. One day she told her father, "If you don't take me to Baba for his *darshan,* I will never ever recover."

Her condition was so precarious that it was a problem to take her so far. Finally her father decided to seek the doctor's advice on this. Unanimously they said, "It's her last wish, she is in the terminal stage, so do take her to Shirdi."

So, her father asked some of his relatives to accompany them.

## Malanbai goes to Shirdi

After they had Baba's *darshan,* he started shouting and using abusive language, then he said, "*तिला घोंगड्यावर टाक व मडक्यातले पाणी पाजून पडू दे।।*"

"Let her lie on a blanket, and give her water from an earthen pot to drink. Let her lie there." Malanbai was taken to Dixit *wada,* there she happily agreed to everything as she had full faith in Baba. For a week she did just that, and then one morning she died. Her grandmother and other relatives started crying, and they consoled each other. The male members went to make funeral arrangements. Sathe Sahib tried his best to console them.

The devotees had gathered in the Dwaraka Mai for *Kakad arati,* but Baba just would not get up. When he did get up he was in a terrible rage. He struck the floor with his *satka* many times. Simultaneously he let out a volley of fowl language and abuses. Then Baba got up and went towards Dixit *wada* in rage. He was abusing and shaking his *satka* at the room where Malanbai stayed.

At that very moment Malanbai moved her limbs and began yawning. She looked around as if confirming where she was. Then she got up and sat down. Her relatives were shocked and confused. Gently they questioned her, as to what had happened.

## The black man (Yama) was no match for my Baba

Then she narrated this *leela:* "I was being carried away by a black ugly-looking man. He was very rough, and he pulled and dragged me. I did not go with him easily, I called my Baba to save me from this demonic person. Of course my Baba came to me and gave that black man a good thrashing. The black man (Yama) was no match for my Baba, so he let go of me. Then my Baba took me to his *Chavdi* where I lay comfortably."

Then Malanbai went on to narrate what the *Chavdi* looked like. Where Baba sat! And where he slept! Every one who heard this was speechless. Malanbai had never ever seen the *Chavdi,* but her description was accurate.

The family was very happy to see the turn of events. With tears of gratitude they thanked Baba and returned home.

Ref: *Sai Leela Aashad Shake 1845. Ank 5. Year 1 (1923)*

*Leela 43:* # Rinanubandh of a Muslim gentleman

A Muslim gentleman once came for Baba's *darshan*. After having *darshan*, he pleaded with Baba to help him. He said, "Baba, I cannot get a licence for 'igniting and blasting with dynamite'. I need this equipment to dig a deep well. I have made several requests to the Collector Sahib but of no avail. This request, I ask you, and no one else, as you are my only refuge, so please help me." Baba said, "All right, let Nana come and I will ask him to give you the licence."

A few days later Nana Sahib came to Shirdi and the Muslim devotee also turned up. He said, "Baba, Nana has arrived. Now you have to tell him to talk to the collector Sahib about the licence." Baba did just that. Nana heard what Baba had to say. Then he told Baba that the gentleman had already applied twice, and at both the times the collector had refused to give the licence. Now he will never get a licence.

Baba said, "Give it *re*. Don't say that he won't get it." Nana said, "On the two previous occasions his application was scrutinised by two officers and unanimously denied. Now there is no chance of him ever getting it. If I talk on his behalf what plausible reason can I give?" Baba replied, "Nana, you talk to the officer. This time he will get the licence."

Then Baba went on to tell this tale: "This Muslim gentleman had kept a box with me a long time ago. Now he is asking for it to be returned. He has no wish to let me keep it. Then what is the point of keeping it. It's best to return it. Why keep it for no reason." Nana said, "Everything you say is always true. But I am sure he will not get the licence even on the third attempt." Finally, Nana said, "All right, since you are asking me, I will talk to the officers." Again Baba said, "Nana, if you recommend him he will get the licence."

## Nana tells the Muslim gentleman to apply again

Nana then told the gentleman to send the application for the third time. He also instructed him of the exact date and time of the hearing. The exact spot that he should stand, and wait. The Muslim did exactly what he was told to do. Late that evening the hearing commenced. The gentleman stood in front of the officer with his application in hand. The officer asked Nana about the need for a licence in this case, as it had already been denied. Nana explained everything to the officer, and added, "The gentleman is here, and he can tell you why he is persisting on getting the licence." The officer then asked him to state the facts himself.

## The Muslim gentleman wishes to pay back the loan

The gentleman said, "I took a loan of 500 rupees from the government, and used it for my farm. Then, I got a notice stating that the interest payments were due on such and such dates. I want to make the payments but I don't have the money. Now I want a loan of the same amount to dig a well. I need a well to water my fields so I get a good yield. The sale of the yield will give me money to pay back the government. So I started digging the well but there were rocks and boulders and I could not make any progress. Hence I am applying for the licence, so I can use the dynamite to blast the rocks that are hindering the progress. This is the reason for the third application, although I have been denied twice." The officer was satisfied with the explanation, and was very impressed that the man wanted to pay the government its dues.

The officer ordered his staff to get the licence made right there and then. When it was ready he signed it, and gave it to the honest gentleman. That was done at once and the Muslim gentleman went home happily.

Nana says, "Where did this man come from all of a sudden, and ask Baba to help him? Why did he give the box to Baba for safe keeping? When did he give Baba the box? Where was the box, and where did Baba keep it? When did he ask Baba to return his box?" Then Nana explains that Baba knew each and every living being. So he knew all about the facts that the man stated in front of the officer. About the parable he infers that the box represents 'a good deed'. In his previous life this man had contact with Baba. He did some good deed, and in this life he is asking for the fruit or result of that deed. The fruit or result of that good deed being Baba's help in procuring the licence. Ref: *Sai Leela Shravan Shake 1848. Ank 6. Year 4 (1926)*

## Leela 44:  Baba comes to her home and fills her box with udi

There was an elderly lady who wished to remain anonymous, for if she published her name it may breed pride. She and her family lived with her brother, and his family. Hence it was a very large household. The lady was about 70 years old; she was spiritual as well as very religious. Her daily routine was filled with doing various *pujas*, rituals and reading numerous religious books. Both the siblings were utterly devoted to Baba. She prayed and performed Baba's *arati* every day.

It so happened that this lady fell ill, and her condition started deteriorating. Though she was lucid most of the time, she would ramble off and on. The lady thought that she would die soon. So she wished to have Baba's *udi* applied to her forehead and to take some orally. She had a small box in which she kept the *udi*. She asked her daughter-in-law to take some *udi* from the box and apply it on her forehead. But the daughter-in-law found the box empty, so she informed the same to the lady.

Disappointed, she contacted her brother, who always carried *udi* with him. But he was out of station, and it would take a few days to procure it from him. Persistently, she cried out, "Why can't you apply some *udi* on my forehead, and put some in my mouth? This is my last wish, I will die soon." Then she turned, and looked towards the *puja* room and said, "Baba before I pass away, I have only one wish, and it is that your *udi* be given to me." After saying this she calmed down and was quiet for some time.

## Look Baba has come, touch his feet and do puja

At about 12 o'clock, she saw Baba entering her home through the front door. Excitedly, she called her daughter-in-law and said, "Look! Baba has come, give him a seat, touch his feet and do *puja*." But the rest of the family couldn't see Baba. And the family thought that she was hallucinating due to her illness. The lady got restless and agitated as they were not honouring Baba. So, she closed her eyes for some time. Then with a great deal of joy and happiness she shouted, "Look! Baba is putting his *udi* in my box, and now he is leaving. Quickly take his *darshan*." The rest of the family couldn't see Baba, and yet again they thought she was hallucinating.

Adamantly she asked them to give her the *udi*. She would not calm down nor would she stop pestering them. At last her daughter-in-law, in order to calm her, went and got the *udi* box. She knew it was empty, but just to satisfy her she opened it. To her utter amazement and astonishment she found it was filled to the brim with *udi*. She applied the *udi* on the lady's forehead, just as she had requested. Needless to say the lady steadily improved and regained her health. Her family realised that she was telling the truth. But there was a great deal of disappointment that the rest of them couldn't have Baba's *darshan*.

The moral of this *leela* is unshakable faith and complete surrender, and then Baba will be with us all the time.

Ref: *Sai Leela Bhadrapad-Margashrish Shake 1848. Ank 10. Year 4 (1926)*

## Leela 45: Babu Dixit and Babu Bhate were good friends

Babu Dixit was Kaka Sahib's elder son, his name was Ram Krishna. When Kaka Sahib made Shirdi his home he brought his family along with him. Baala Sahib also came to stay in Shirdi; his elder son was also called Babu. Both the children went to the Marathi school in Shirdi. The children were of the same age, and were in the same class at school. They did their homework together, and became good friends. On the days that Baba slept in the *Chavdi*, these youngsters would don *zari toopies* (gold-or silver-trimmed hats) and pretend they were Baba's *chopdars*. They would hold a stick and stand at the entrance of the *Chavdi*, and give *lalkari* (salutations), saying, "*Aalbeli Sarkar aaram kaari*" (Take rest now, unique Majesty).

Baala Bhate was a *Mamlatdar* (well placed government official), but after he came in contact with Baba he resigned from his job. He made Shirdi his home, and dedicated his life to Baba's *seva*. His friends forced him to apply for pension but he did not receive a lot of money because the duration of his service was short. He and his family lived in poverty. Baala spent his time reading and studying religious books. Consequently his face had a lustre on it. Dixit liked Bhate very much, and they read the *Bhagwat* and other books together. Both were utterly devoted to Baba.

Dixit not only educated and looked after Baala's children, but took care of the whole family after Baala's death.

When both the children completed their education at Shirdi, they had to go to the city for higher studies. Kaka after consulting with Baala Bhate sent both the children along with his wife to Mumbai. They did their schooling there, and later went to Benaras Central Hindu College. Bhate chose to do B.A. while Dixit joined the B.Sc.

stream. Both were bright and hard working and passed with good grades. Bhate wished to do M.A. and Law, but his father died, and the responsibility of taking care of his mother and younger brother fell on his shoulders. So he gave up the idea of studying further, and took up a job in a bank. Bhate was ever so grateful to Kaka Dixit for educating him, and did not want to be a burden on him any further. The bank gave him a salary of Rs 100/- and with that meagre amount he took care of his Mother, and educated his younger brother.

Kaka Dixit's kindness and compassion extended far beyond his family. He and his wife, whom every one lovingly called Bhabi Saibha, treated Babu Bhate like their own son. Whatever was given to their Babu, was also given to Bhate, be it food, or clothing. Their home at Vile Parle was infested with scorpions, and often snakes would crawl on the floor. So iron cots were bought, and given to both of them.

Babu Bhate was hard working, honest and a responsible man. When his younger brother completed his schooling he wanted him to pursue higher education. So his younger brother joined a college for postgraduation. During that time Bapu Bhate went to Nasik on official duty, there he contracted cholera and died.

Ref: *Sai Leela Margashrish Shake 1857. Ank 6-9. Year 12*


## Leela 46:  Nana looks at a Muslim lady

This *leela* is given in *Shri Sai Satcharita*, Chapter 49. More details are given below.

On one of his visits to Shirdi, Nana Sahib Chandorkar was sitting with Baba in the sanctum sanctorum of the Dwaraka Mai and conversing with him. There he noticed two Muslim ladies in the *sabhamandap* below waiting to have Baba's *darshan*. Since they had been waiting for quite a long time and were hesitant to come up,

Nana thought, 'I have been sitting here for a long time. They want to have Baba's *darshan* but are shy to come up because I am sitting here'.

He was about to get up when Baba said, "Where are you going? And why are you leaving?" Nana explained the reason for leaving. Then Baba said, "Sit down! Don't go any where, there is no reason for you to leave. If those women have an urge and need to have *darshan* they will come up. If they were so shy then why do they come for *darshan*?" Nana said not a word and sat down.

They were *pardha-clad* women. Hence they waited a little more, and when Nana was still sitting there, they came up. They bowed to Baba, and laid their head on Baba's feet. While doing so they lifted the veil. One of them was an elderly lady, she bowed first. The younger lady then bowed and lifted her veil. Nana casually looked at her. She was young and extremely beautiful. He thought, 'If only she would lift her veil again, so I can see her once more'.

The thought had just crossed his mind when Baba slapped him on his thigh. After *darshan* the ladies sat for a while and then left. As soon as they left, Baba said, "Nana, do you know the reason of my slapping you on the thigh?" Nana said, "Baba you are the 'all knowing' *sadguru*. I can't steal and hide any thing from you, as you are bound to know it. But what I cannot understand is that when I am next to you how could the mind seek passion?"

Then Baba explained in detail about human nature and passion. Baba said, "Nana, aren't you a human being? The human being is filled with passion. This passion will awake and rise time and again.

"There are myriad of beautifully carved temples. One temple is more beautiful and awesome than the other. But when we go to these temples do we dwell on the beauty of the architecture, or the outer facade? We enter the temple and behold the exquisitely carved idol. Again we don't dwell on the beauty of the idol, but look at its divinity.

"Then shouldn't we appreciate the ingenuity and skill of Brahmdev? How skillful he is to create this Universe, so vast and beautiful. Then we realise that God resides in each and every atom of this universe, be it beautiful or ugly.

"Nana, when you see a beautiful human being, you should think how god resides in this beautiful person. This will make you appreciate the beauty without being disturbed. If you saw the same Muslim lady after having heard this, you would not have wanted to see her again.

"Remember this for ever. Live in this world, as you have always done, but try to think of ways to make these passions weak. Then turn you mind towards attaining your spiritual goal."

Thus Baba gave a wonderful dissertation on passion and leading normal life.           Ref: *Sai Leela Shravan Shake 1848. Ank 6. Year 4*

## Leela 47: Govindpanth N Chandorkar forbids his family to have any contact with Muslims

Nana Sahib Chandorkar was a deputy collector and so was his father, before he retired. His father's name was Govindpanth Nana Chandorkar. His father had worked in that very office before Nana. So when referring to the senior Chandorkar they said *daftadar* (officer). People referred to the building as *daftar* and his home as *daftardar's wada*. They called the junior Chandorkar, Nana Sahib.

Nana Sahib was well educated, and had travelled widely. He had a lot of Muslim friends from school, college and at work. His father however was narrow minded. Once he had a disagreement with a Muslim, so he forbade every one in the family from talking to, or having any sort of relations with any Muslim. The family implicitly obeyed his orders.

Nana, however, was on official duty at that time and was out of station. His father did have a lot of Muslim friends through Nana's cordial relationship with them. Subsequently, Govindpanth learned to accept them. But because of the disagreement, this order was passed by him. When Nana returned, everyone told him what had happened.

Nana was devoted to his father, and obeyed whatever he said. Now he was upset, for if he obeyed his father's words, he would lose many of his Muslim friends. On the other hand if he did not obey his father it would be an insult to him. Finally he decided to lay all his problems before his father, and listen to what he has to say. But Baba in his unique way solved the problem for him.

## Baba grips Govindpanth's mind and allows Nana to worship Baba

He asked for a meeting with his father. When they met he said, "I am going to lay all my problems before you. I have no problem with not talking to my Muslim friends, but there is one big hurdle for me. Shri Sai Baba is a self-realised Muslim saint. He resides at Shirdi, which is in Kopergaon *talluqa*, in Ahmednagar. Baba is my guru, and I go often to meet him. If I follow your order and do not go to meet him, it will be detrimental to my spiritual growth. I know your guru is Shri Samarth Shakaram Maharaj and he is a Brahmin. This is a big problem for me."

Calmly his father replied, "Even if Shri Sai Baba is a Muslim, you must continue going to him. Shri Shakaram though a Brahmin, is my guru, but not yours. So you must go to your guru." Nana was astonished to hear this. He was overcome with joy and tears rolled down his cheeks. He mentally thanked Baba for changing his father's mind. He wondered when this change happened.

Ref: *Sai Leela Aashad Shake 1848. Ank 6. Year 4 (1923)*

Whenever Nana Sahib visited Shirdi, Baba gave him a palmful of *udi*. This *udi* Nana stored in a safe place, and gave it to devotees when they were very sick. He always carried this round box full of *udi* and a small photograph of Baba wherever he went. And indeed no harm befell him. This box and photograph is now with his grandson, Prabhakar, who resides in Pune.

# Leela 48:    These people are walking all over me

Eager to have their *sadguru's darshan* on *Gurupurnima* day, the devotees flocked to Shirdi. They came from far and near, some did *padyatra* (walking on a pilgrimage). Others came by *tonga*, or bullock cart, and yet many others came by rail. Every devotee hoped to receive that special blessing from Baba. Bearing gifts of flowers, garlands, fruits, sweets and shawls they came to the Dwaraka Mai. Some devotees brought books hoping that Baba would sanctify the book with his touch and return it, so that they could read it and benefit from it.

Others brought photographs of Baba, hoping to receive the photograph back as *prasad* so that they could worship it. They all rushed to the Dwaraka Mai trying to get Baba's *darshan*. The *sabhamandap* was packed to suffocation with the devotees eager to get into the sanctum sanctorum.

Baba suddenly turned to Jyotindra and said, "These people are walking all over me. I feel pain as they stamp on me. Bhau, (Baba called Jyotindra 'Bhau') go and rescue me." Jyotindra was surprised to hear this as Baba was sitting near the railing in his usual place.

Then pushing him gently, Baba pointed in a certain direction and said, "Go and rescue me. Some one has dropped a photograph of mine. It's on the floor and people are walking on it." Then Jyotindra said, "Baba, the crowd is overwhelming. If I go there, they will crush me in the stampede." Baba assured him that nothing would happen to him as he was under his protection. Jyotindra followed Baba's instructions and slowly made his way in that direction. Finally, he reached almost to the end of the *sabhamandap*, there he found Baba's photograph on the ground. Some devotee had dropped the photograph. The other devotees in their enthusiasm to reach Baba were treading on it.

He picked up the photograph and brought it to Baba. With a look of relief on his face Baba gave the photograph to Jyotindra. "Preserve this photograph," said Baba. This small photograph is still in the Tarkhad home. It is venerated and prayed to daily.

Ref: *As narrated by Jyotindra's son Virendra Tarkhad*

## Leela 49: He calls Baba to save his staff from a catastrophe at work

G B Mankar was an engineering contractor by profession. His assignment for that day was to stand a very heavy machine upright, with the aid of a crane. He and his staff were at the job site. The machine to be lifted had a 375 horse power diesel engine. Its 'fly pulley' weighed about 12 tons. He was not aware that the crane being used was not equipped to lift such a heavy and large weight.

The crane was fitted to the fly pulley and was being heaved, when he heard a loud noise of the crane cracking. His heart sank and was frightened out of his wits, and he perspired profusely. For if the crane broke, then all his workers would be crushed to death. He shouted at the top of his voice, "Baba! now come and save every body here." No sooner had the words come out of his mouth, the job site was pervaded with the fragrance of roses and incense. At once he knew Baba was there, and his heart was filled with joy.

The staff was oblivious of the impending catastrophe and were wondering where the fragrance of roses was coming from. "Who is burning incense?" they asked. Mankar with a heart bursting with gratitude said, "All right! My Baba has come." They wondered at their employer's words. He had called out to his father. The word

Baba is usually used to refer to one's father or an elderly person. The employees looked around but Mankar's father was not there. They asked him where his father was. Mankar laughed and said, "By saying Baba, I mean Shri Sai Baba."

Then the operation went on smoothly, and the machinery was lifted and placed properly. At this time words cannot convey what Mankar felt. He was crying and laughing at the same time. Due to Baba's presence a major catastrophe was averted.

Ref: *Sai Leela Aashad Shake 1825. Ank 5. Year 1*

## Leela 50: Captain Vir Hate gets his rupee blessed by Baba

The story of Captain Vir Hate and the one rupee is given in *Shri Sai Satcharita*, Chapter 29. Some more details are given below.

Dr Hate was a staunch devotee of Baba, and stayed in Shirdi for some time. Then he returned to Gwalior where he resided. One day Sallu Ram came to him and informed him that his son was missing for a while now. He, his wife and daughter-in-law had made a through search but were unable to locate him. Dr Hate advised him to go to Shirdi, saying, "Baba will definitely tell you his whereabouts." Sallu Ram took a vow, saying, "If I hear from or about my son, I will go to Shirdi."

A few days later he received a letter from his son. His son had left home and secretly joined the army as he feared his parents' wrath. He was posted to Egypt, but now he was returning home. He informed Dr Hate about it, and again he told him to go and have Baba's *darshan*. Sallu agreed, but instead of going to Shirdi he went to Bombay to meet his son.

Sallu Ram, his wife and daughter-in-law went to Bombay to welcome him. Sallu Ram was happy to see his son, but the condition of his son was upsetting. The boy was running a high fever and was emaciated. He at once took his son to Dr Hate for treatment in Gwalior. Dr Hate said, "Time and again I told you to go to Shirdi but you did not go. Now take your son to Shirdi and lay him at Baba's feet. He will definitely recover." This time Sallu Ram did just that.

Before they left, Dr Hate gave Sallu Ram a rupee coin and said, "Place this rupee in Baba's hand. He will return it, so I can keep it in my prayer room as his *prasad*. Don't forget to bring it back." Sallu Ram agreed and he and his family finally went to Shirdi. Before leaving he asked Dr Hate for a letter of introduction, but Dr Hate told him that it was not necessary.

They had Baba's *darshan* and his son started recuperating. He then placed the coin in Baba's hand. Baba returned the coin saying, "Give this coin back to the owner."

The family returned to Gwalior and Sallu Ram told Dr Hate everything that had happened. Then he handed over the coin that Baba had blessed. Dr Hate took it in his hand but felt that it was not his coin. Sallu Ram returned home and told his wife about it. She, however, just went inside and brought the original coin which she had put away safely. The next day a thrilled Dr Hate received the coin (*prasad*). Sallu Ram apologised for the substitution, and Dr Hate forgave him.                    Ref: *Sai Leela Aashad Shake 1846. Ank 3. Year 2*

## Baba rescues Captain Daruwalla from the enemy attack

❝I may be here in my physical body, and you may be far away beyond the seven seas, yet, whatever you do there I know instantly. Wherever you may be, when you spread your hands before me in supplication with faith and devotion, there I stand behind you day and night steadfast as your faith and devotion," said Baba to Cholkar in *Shri Sai Satcharita* Chapter 15, *Ovi* 67.

Baba's words are true for each and every devotee even now, as they were then. This is such a *leela* where Baba literally goes beyond the seven seas to rescue a devotee.

It was during the Russo-Japanese War of 1905; Captain Jahanghir F Daruwalla was at sea with his fleet of ships. To his utter dismay he realised that all but three of his ships were hit by the enemy and were sinking fast. Soon these three ships with passengers, crew, and himself would meet the same fate. Being a good captain, he hoped to ferry the remaining ships to safety.

He had a photograph of Baba in his pocket. He promptly took it out and earnestly prayed to Baba to come to their rescue. Just as he was praying, Baba sitting in the Dwaraka Mai shouted, "Haq, haq." The devotees sitting with Baba were astounded to see him completely drenched from head to toe. Water flowed in torrents, and soon the Dwaraka Mai became a pool of water. For about an hour the devotees removed buckets and buckets of water. Then they gave Baba a dry *kafni* to wear.

As Baba was silent about the cause of his being drenched, one of the devotees drank the water as *tirth* (holy water) and found it extremely salty. Simultaneously, at sea Captain Daruwalla saw Baba in person pull and tow his ships to safety. On the third day after this incident Baba received a telegram from the Captain, thanking him for the rescue operation.

When he returned home after completion of his mission, he came to Shirdi and prostrated at Baba's feet. He thanked Baba for answering his prayers so swiftly, and saving the lives of his crew and the passengers.

Captain Daruwalla was an ardent devotee and took a great deal of interest in Baba's affairs. He donated Rs 2,200/- in two installments for repairing the *sabhamandap* of the Dwaraka Mai. This was a small 'thank you' gesture.

## Leela 52: **This lady from Poona wishes to get a coconut from Baba**

"Do coconuts produce children? How can you be so superstitious? People seem to have gone crazy," said Baba to Shama in *Shri Sai Satcharita* Chapter 36, *Ovi 150*. Shama was pleading with Baba on behalf of Mrs Aurangabadkar. He beseeched Baba to give her the blessed coconut, so that the barren lady might conceive and get a child. "She will get a child in 12 months," said Baba.

This is another coconut *leela*.

There was a lady residing in Poona. Though married for many years she did not have any children. This made her extremely sad and she thought, 'If only Baba gave me a coconut I will surely have children'. So she tried to go to Shirdi, but every time she was to leave for Shirdi some problem came up and she had to cancel her trip. This made her very sad. From her very soul she felt that if she got a coconut from Baba her wish would be fulfilled. She tried various ways and means to go to Shirdi but did not succeed.

One night with a very heavy heart she went to sleep. That night, she dreamt of Baba. He gave her a coconut, and there ended the dream. The dream was so real that she got up and looked around for the coconut. Lo! the coconut was near her pillow. Surprised but happy, she took the coconut and vowed, saying, "Baba, if I get a male child after eating this coconut I will bring the child to Shirdi and lay him at your feet."

With Baba's grace she delivered a boy. When the child was two months, she came to Shirdi and laid the child at Baba's feet. She thanked him for his infinite mercy.

Ref: *Sai Leela Aashad Shake 1846. Ank 3. Year 2 (1924)*

## Leela 53: Baba restores the eye sight of Vitthal's grandfather

Vitthal Yashwant Deshpande lived with his parents and grandparents in Dadar, Mumbai. A tragedy brought him to Baba's feet. His grandfather suddenly fell sick and gradually lost his sight. All sorts of remedies, treatments, doctors and *vaids* were tried but to no avail and he gradually became totally blind. Vitthal was very fond of his grandfather and helped him to move around in the house.

There lived in Bandra a *satpurush* (saintly man) named, Govind Rao Mankar. He was a devotee of Sai Baba. He met Vitthal's grandfather and advised him to go to Shirdi, and seek Baba's blessings for a cure. The grandfather was impressed by the *satpurush*, and was determined to go to Shirdi. Time and again a trip was planned, but for some reason or the other the trip was postponed.

### Vitthal takes his grandfather to Shirdi
In 1916, Vitthal was just twelve years old. As his uncle was busy, it was decided that Vitthal would take his grandfather to Shirdi. Before leaving, his parents repeatedly told Vitthal to behave properly and

take care of his grandfather. They reached Shirdi and went to the Dwaraka Mai. They took *darshan* and prostrated before Baba. "Give me Rs 6/- as *dakshina*," said Baba. Vitthal thrust his hand into his pocket and found that he had a ten rupee, and a five rupee note. He gave Baba the 10 rupee note, which he did not accept. Neither would he accept the 5 rupee note nor would he give him change. Vitthal tried again with the same result. "Give me Rs 6," said Baba.

So Vitthal brought his grandfather to the *sabhamandap* below, and seated him in a corner next to the wall. Vitthal then went out to get the change. But try as he may, no one gave him change. Frustrated, and wondering how his grandfather was, he started crying.

## A benefactor helps him

Suddenly a well-built man stood before him. He had on a clean *dhotar* (Indian dress), a *pagdi* (turban) and Poona shoes (shoes with a curled toe). His forehead was smeared with sandalwood paste. Gently he asked, "Child, why are you crying?" Vitthal told him how stubborn Baba was, and his inability to get change. Quietly he gave him the change.

Vitthal ran to the Dwaraka Mai and placed 6 rupees at Baba's feet. Baba said, "*Daaro mat beta, Allah accha karega. Ab tumahra kaam hogaya*" (Do not fear my child. Allah will do good. Now your work is done.) Vitthal was astonished, but rather confused. He had not told Baba why he had come, nor had Baba asked. He just stood there staring at Baba. Baba repeated the same words again. Still confused he went to the corner where he had seated his grandfather, but he was not there. He searched in the *sabhamandap*, but couldn't find him. So he ran through the village, calling his grandfather, but he couldn't find him.

Dejected and afraid, he started crying bitterly. He wondered if his grandfather had fallen or hurt himself. Lo! the same man stood before him. "Why are you crying now?" he asked gently. Through sobs Vitthal told him what had happened. "Your grandfather is seated on the steps of Sathe *wada*," he said pointing in that direction. Vitthal ran and found his grandfather happily eating sugar cane.

Upset and frustrated, he said, "Why did you leave the place I made you sit? Suppose you fell and hurt yourself. How did you reach here?" His grandfather told him that as soon as he went to get the change, his sight started returning. "By the time you came back I could see clearly. So I came to the *wada*." Vitthal was relieved to hear this.

## Baba asks for dakshina

Baba insisted that Vitthal give him Rs 6/- as *dakshina*. This could mean giving unto Baba the 6 internal enemies (lust, anger, greed, delusion, pride and envy.) These thrive on the 5 senses (sight, hearing, speech, smell and taste). In *Shri Sai Satcharita* Chapter 16, *Shadripus* is explained.

On the way back home, Vitthal lost his cap, and was afraid to tell his grandfather about it. Finally, they reached Dadar. His parents were waiting for their arrival. When he turned around, his grandfather was missing. He collected their bags and walked slowly towards his parents. They eagerly questioned him about the trip. He mumbled something, just then his grandfather arrived with a new cap. Vitthal was filled with immense joy as he finally got proof that his grandfather could really see.

'But who was the mysterious gentleman, and how did he know who my grandfather was?' he wondered.

Ref: *Sai Sagar Deepavali Ank. Year 2001*

Vitthal often visited Shirdi, and after Baba's *Mahasamadhi* he made it a point to attend the three major festivals. Vitthal never left Shirdi without Baba's permission. He had a unique way of doing this. When it was time for him to leave Shirdi, he went to the *Samadhi* Mandir and placed a coconut on the *padukas*. Then he bowed his head on the *padukas*, saying, "Baba, I am returning home with your permission."

Once Vitthal and two other devotees (Dammu Anna Rasne and Shakaram Schinde) left Shirdi without Baba's permission. They were in a hurry as Dammu Anna had an important meeting to attend. The vehicle was Schinde's car, and he was driving it. They had nearly reached Nagar when a cobbler on a bicycle came in front of the vehicle. A terrible accident occurred, were the cobbler was thrown off his bike and he sustained a head injury. He lost consciousness, and there was no water to give the injured man. But they did have Baba's *udi*, so they gave it to him, and he regained consciousness. They took him to the hospital and there it came to light that he had a broken thigh bone. Subsequently, he became all right and was discharged.

This was a lesson for all of them; Vitthal never again left Shirdi without Baba's permission.  Ref: *Sai Sagar Deepavali Ank. Year 2001*

*Leela 54:*  # Chandrabai Borker was devoted to Baba

Chandrabai's husband was posted to a small town called Aaswali near Nasik. One day her husband (Ramchandra Borker) returned from work with a high fever. Chandrabai was extremely worried as there were no doctors nearby, nor was medical aid easily available. Chandrabai had some of Baba's *udi* with her. She had immense faith in Baba and knew that the *udi* was a panacea for all maladies. She made her husband as comfortable as she possibly could, and sat beside him. The temperature was 103°F and was steadily rising. At about 2 a.m. her husband fell asleep so she curled up at the foot of the bed and took a nap.

**The kafni clad Fakir warns her about impending danger**
At 3 o'clock in the morning she had a vivid dream. In the dream she saw an old *kafni-clad* fakir, who said, "Bai, don't be worried. In a little while he will perspire profusely. Just apply *udi* all over him and his fever will abate. However do not let him go out of the house after 11 o'clock." Then the fakir disappeared. She followed his instructions; her husband was sweating profusely at that time. She wiped off the perspiration and applied the *udi*. Then she told her husband about the dream, but her husband lacked faith in Baba.

80

Not heeding her advice, he went out to the railway station which was very close to their house. At that time the passenger train going to Mumbai had just arrived. From her home she could see her husband standing on the tracks and talking to his friend. The Mail arriving from Manmad was approaching on that track to the station. Her husband was oblivious of the oncoming train. Chandrabai from her home watched the train hit her husband. She shouted, "Baba" and lost her consciousness.

## Baba saves her husband from a horrible death

A shortwhile later, a porter came to her home, and told her to bring her husband home, as he had broken a bone or two. She immediately thanked Baba for saving her husband's life. So she along with a servant went to the platform. A lot of people who had witnessed the accident were marvelling how the train instead of running over him, had knocked him on the middle track that was empty at that time.

Chandrabai brought her husband home and laid him on the bed. The pain was severe for he kept losing consciousness off and on. In his groggy state, he said, "Where am I? A fakir has stealthily crept into our home." Chandrabai reassured him, saying, "That fakir is our Baba. He is our only refuge but you do not have faith in him, for you would not have gone out after I told you about the dream. It for was a warning, but you did not pay any heed to it. Nonetheless he saved your life, or I would have been crying as you would have lost your life. Time and again you promised to go to Shirdi but every time you reneged on your promise. At least this time I hope you keep your promise to go, after you recover." Her husband finally promised to do so. Then he said, "Is your Baba in Shirdi now?" Chandrabai replied, "Yes, he is in Shirdi and also with me. Otherwise you would have been run over by the train."

Chandrabai tended to his leg, obviously it was broken. She took some *udi* and mixed it with a powder of *biba* (marking nut). She put it over the injured part, and then bandaged it. The next day the doctor from the Railway Hospital came and checked her husband and confirmed that there was a fracture.

## The kafni-clad fakir instructs her about treating her husband

That night at 11 p.m. she dreamt of the same fakir who asked, "So what has happened? The leg is broken? Get some *khobra* (desiccated coconut) and place it over the injury and bandage it tightly. Then make a mixture of *vaani* (an indigenous fruit), salt, turmeric and *zondhale* (Javari grain). And ferment the bandaged area." Chandrabai did just that. Soon the pain decreased and by the end of the month the fracture had healed perfectly. The doctor and many of her friends and relatives were astonished to see the result of her homemade remedy. She told them that the fakir had advised her to do so, and their faith in Baba increased manifold.

Ref: *Sai Leela Margashrish Shake 1847. Ank 9. Year 3 (1925)*

Chandrabai first visited Shirdi in 1892, and had the opportunity to witness many divine *leelas*. This further strengthened her faith, love and devotion for Baba. Baba lovingly called her 'Bai' and asked her to stay in the home of some devotee whenever she visited Shirdi.

## Baba gave Chandrabai udi and blessed her

Every day after *arati* Baba gave her *udi* and blessed her. This *udi* she collected in a box and preserved it in her home. Fully aware of its power and potency she used it sparingly but wisely. But readily gave it to the sick and infirm devotees. Baba also gave her his tooth; she made a talisman of it and venerated it. On another occasion Baba gave her a small portrait of his painted by Shamrao Jaiker. With intense faith and devotion she prayed to it. This portrait is still in her home at Vile Parle, Mumbai, and is cared for by her descendants.

## Baba grants her wish to have a baby

On one of her visits to Shirdi, in 1918, Baba asked her, "Bai, what is your heart's desire? Ask for it and it will be granted." Without hesitation she replied, "Baba, you are *antaryami*. What can I tell you that you don't already know?" At that time she was 48 years old but she yearned to have a child, but had never asked Baba to grant her the wish.

Her friends, family and doctors alike declared that conception was impossible at her age. Chandrabai, however, was full of *shradha* and *saburi*, she knew nothing was impossible with Baba. Time rolled by and three years later her menses stopped. About five months later she noticed that her stomach was bloated and she was vomiting every morning. This was accompanied with swelling of her feet.

Dr Purandhare (the famous gynaecologist) diagnosed her to have a tumor of the uterus. He advised her to have a surgery immediately and get it removed. Chandrabai refused to have surgery and said, "I will bide my 10 months and then decide." Dr Purandhare patiently explained to her that at fifty-one, and after a long and continued absence of conception, pregnancy was impossible. She adamantly said that she was pregnant. During that period her physical condition gradually deteriorated. The only medicines that Chandrabai took were *udi* and water, for about 5 months.

On *dhanatrayodashi* a son was born, i.e., 3 years and 2 days after Baba's *mahaniryan*. She continued doing her household chores up to the time of delivery. To the surprise of every one she had a safe and easy delivery, without the aide of a doctor, nurse or medications.

*Leela 55:* # She was a sister of mine for seven births

"Wherever I go she comes searching for me. She was my sister for seven generations," said Baba to Dixit about Chandrabai.

In July 1918, Chandrabai visited Shirdi. Baba turned to her and said, "Bai, you need not take the trouble to come and see me here henceforth. I am with you wherever you are." His love and compassion overwhelmed her and she broke into tears. After getting *udi* from Baba she went to Panchgani. Although it was a serene and beautiful place, she was restless.

One day she got a letter from Kaka Dixit, stating that Baba was often thinking of her. And that Baba's health was rapidly deteriorating.

Immediately she went to Shirdi, and was there when Baba took *mahaniryan*. She was fortunate to give him some water at the last moment, as did Nimonkar. Then Baba leaned on Bayyaji's shoulder and took *samadhi*.

The descendants of Chandrabai still live in Vile Parle, Mumbai. She built a beautiful temple of her *ista dev* (Sai Baba) adjacent to her home. This temple is unique as it houses an idol of Baba in the famous 'Dwaraka Mai' pose. With great devotion, daily *puja* with all the rituals are performed there.

On one of her visits to Shirdi, Baba gave her a small *satka* (*sanyasi's* staff). With utter devotion it is venerated.

*Leela 56:* # Nana Sahib Chandorkar's son's wedding in Gwalior

This *leela* is given in *Shri Sai Satcharita* Chapter 46. Here some more details are given. The wedding of Nana Sahib's son was to be held at Gwalior. Dixit reached there in the evening, a day prior to the wedding. Nana welcomed him and told him that the next morning they would go to meet the guru of their friend, Chintamanrao Vaidya. Nana was very keen to invite him to the wedding.

Early next morning the three of them (Nana, Dixit and, Shama, who had arrived a few days ago) set out. The first part of the journey was by train. While the second part was by bullock cart. They reached the station, whence the final leg of the journey was to be taken. At the station there was only one *tonga*, eagerly they sat in it. But when they told the driver their destination, he said, "You better get down as my horses will not be able to take you that far." So they started looking for another *tonga*. Dixit told Nana that they had better return, as the *muhurath* (auspicious time) for the wedding was not too far off.

Bapu Sahib Jog's *samadhi* in Sakori
(Leela 14)

Photograph taken with Baba's consent
(Leela 28)

*Padukas* given to Nachne by Baba
(Leela 32)

Shantaram Balwant Nachne
(Leela 32)

कै. विष्णु बळवंत पितळे व कै. राधाबाई विष्णु पितळे

Vishnupanth B Pithale and
Radhabai Pithale (Leela 33)

Baba hugged this photograph and
returned it to Vishnupanth Pithale
(Leela 33)

Tulsi Brindavan,
Bhivpuri Road Mandir (Leela 34)

Bass relief replica of Baba at
Bhivpuri Road (Leela 34)

Keshev R Pradhan (Leela 34)

Bhivpuri Road Mandir (Leela 34)

Dev Baba alias
Ananth Prabhu Walvalkar (Leela 35)

Dattatreya Deshpande Nimonkar
(Leela 36)

"Take this photo home and everything
of yours will become gold"
(Leela 37)

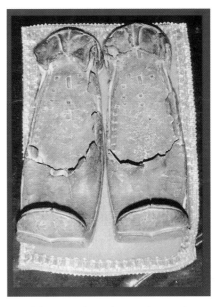

*Padukas* given by Baba to Chottu Bhaya
(Leela 37)

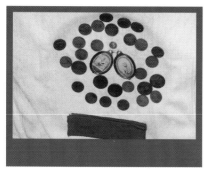

The locket that Baba kissed (Leela 38)

Seetadevi Tarkhad (Leela 39)

Jyotindra R Tarkhad (Leela 40)

Baba's photograph in Jyotindra's home
(Leela 41)

Sandalwood *devera* in Jyotindra's home
(Leela 41)

Ram Krishna Dixit alias Bapu
(Leela 45)

Baba's pocket, silver *padukas*, gold and other
coins given by Baba to Jyotindra Tarkhad
(Leela 47)

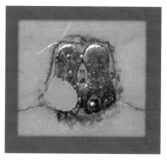

*Udi* box and Baba's photograph belonging to
Chandorkar (Leela 47)

Silver *padukas* of Baba given to
Jyotindra Tarkhad (Leela 48)

"Preserve this Photo"
said Baba to Jyotindra Tarkhad
(Leela 48)

Vitthal Yashwant Deshpande
(Leela 53)

Ramchandra Borker (Leela 54)

Chandrabai Borker (Leela 54)

Baba's idol in the temple built by
Chandrabai Borker (Leela 55)

Shri Sai Baba Mandir, Kohrale (Leela 72)

Original *padukas* of Baba at Kohrale Mandir
(Leela 72)

Madhav Nath Maharaj
(Leela 73)

*Vaishvadev* or *Agni dev*
(Leela 76)

*Audumbar* tree in front of Hanuman Mandir, Rui
(Leela 83)

Hanuman Mandir, Rui
(Leela 83)

Hanuman's idol in
Rui Temple (Leela 83)

(1) (Left) Bhaskar Sapatnekar
(2) (Middle) Murlidhar Sapatnekar
(3) (Right) Dinkar Sapatnekar
(Leela 86)

Baba's *kafni* given to
Gavankar (Leela 87)

Dr Keshev Bhagvan
Gavankar (Leela 87)

*Bhakari* (Leela 87)

Baba sent this portrait
to Sadu Bhayia's home
on 8-2-1915 (Leela 90)

Plague infested home of
Sadu Bhayia (Leela 90)

Laxman Rao (Leela 91)

Silver *padukas* given by Das Ganu to
Mina Tai (Leela 93)

Silver *padukas* given by Baba to Mrs Oke
(Leela 94)

श्री.मच्छिंद्रनाथ मंदीर
मच्छिंद्रनाथ गड

Machindragad (Leela 98)

मच्छिंद्रगडावरील
श्री.मच्छिंद्रनाथांची समाधी

*Samadhi* of Machindra Nath
(Leela 98)

Nana however was adamant to go; he said, "Kaka, there is no reason for me to return now. The marriage can take place without me. Besides I took Baba's permission to invite guruji, and he readily gave it. Now no matter what, I will go and invite him." As they were thus speaking a *tonga* turned up and they were on their way.

The roads were bad and were getting worse. Nana thought that the distance to be covered was 5 miles, but it was 5 *Kos*. One *Kos* is about 2 miles. The horses were tired, and they stopped and rested very often. Finally, they reached their destination.

They had a wonderful *darshan* of Guruji, who blessed them. He gave them *udi*, saying, "This is Lord Hari's *udi*." Then they left after inviting him. The return journey was even worse; they lost their way and were very late. They would now miss the train. But this did not happen. By the grace of Baba, they did board the train; they also found plenty of fruits. So they were able to have *faral* (a meal of fruits usually eaten during fasts).

They finally reached the wedding *pandal* (tent), and about 15 minutes later the wedding ceremonies took place.

Ref: *Sai Leela Aashad Shake 1846. Ank 3. Year 2 (1924)*

## Leela 57:   Kaka Dixit extends monetary help to a friend

Kaka Dixit was kind and compassionate by nature. Once, a friend of his was in need of money. At that time Dixit was short of money. He thought to himself that if he could get the payment that was pending; he would surely help his friend. But he was not sure whether his friend would accept his help. He wondered how he could give him the money, without his refusal.

As soon as he received the money he put some of it in an envelope along with a letter and decided to send it to his friend. But Baba had told him not to give anyone money without his permission. Besides Kaka never ever did anything without first consulting Baba.

He took the envelope and the letter to the Dwaraka Mai and asked Baba, "Baba, can I send this letter?" Baba said, "Yes." So Dixit sent it, his friend received it and accepted it.

That evening Dixit met his friend, who said, "Two hours before I received your letter, Baba appeared and said this to my wife, 'I will be coming to your house today. Tell your husband not to be rude to me.' That gave me an indication that I would receive your letter."

Ref: *Sai Leela Jyeshth Shake 1846. Ank 3. Year 2 (1924)*

## Leela 58: The 'bhils' are afraid of the fakir

In 1914, Ganpath Ghondu Kadam and his family were going to Shirdi. They were travelling by train on the Nasik route. About two stations ahead of Nasik, fifteen to twenty well-built *bhils* boarded the train. They entered the compartment while the train was moving. Kadam and his family were the lone passengers in that compartment. At that time Kadam was reading a book called *Bhakti Marg Pradeep* written by Lakshman R Pangarkar. He was reading it aloud to his family.

Some of the *bhils* sat close to him; he thought that they were interested in listening to what he was reading. So he raised his voice a little and read to them. They sat there for about five minutes or so. Then they left and alighted while the train was still running. Kadam got up and went to the door, and he found them fleeing. As he returned to his seat he noticed an elderly fakir seated in front of him.

Quite surprised to see him, Kadam wondered, as to when this Fakir entered his compartment? And how he boarded a moving train? He was deep in thought, after a while he looked up and the Fakir was not there. Astounded, he looked every where for him, but he had disappeared.

They reached Shirdi, and went to the Dwaraka Mai. There Baba said, "So you have reached safely?" Then it dawned upon him that the fakir was Baba. The *bhils* were dacoits who had intended to rob him, so they were sitting next to him. But they were deterred by the presence of the fakir, so they fled from there.

He laid his head on Baba's feet, and thanked him for his protection.          Ref: *Sai Leela Aashad Shake 1846. Ank 3. Year 2 (1924)*

*Leela 59:*       # The avaricious bhajan mandali from Madras

In *Shri Sai Satcharita* Chapter 29, the *leela* of the avaricious *bhajan mandali* from Madras is given. Some of the details like their names, addresses and other particulars are missing. The *leela* given below elaborates on it.

He was called Bhau Swamy because his Guru was Ram Bhau from south Kanara. His real name was Govinda Swamy, and he worked for Madras Electric Tramways. He and his family went on an all India pilgrimage in 1915. They visited Shirdi on 23-8-1915. They sang beautifully and did *bhajans*. Baba gave them Rs 2/- and *burfi* worth Rs 2/-. They sold the *burfi* for one rupee and twelve *annas*. All these details he wrote in his diary daily.

One day he had a dream vision of Baba (which is elaborated in *Shri Sai Satcharita*). After this revealing vision, the greedy sceptic became an ardent devotee. Dr Pillai asked him to write about his dream, which he did and handed it over to him. Knowing of Radha Krishna

Mai's love for *bhajans* he did *bhajans* in her home too. She gave him a Marathi book on the life of Sai Baba, which he treasured.

Bhau Swamy's wife, Adilashmiamal, was given a *sakshatkar* (vision) of Shri Ram at the noon *arati*, while the rest of the *mandali* saw Baba sitting in his usual place. Filled with joy she decided to make *prasad* of *bhaji* and *pyasam* (Indian savouries) for Baba. On 30-8-1915 while preparing it she fervently prayed to Baba to accept it. As she had prepared it with love and devotion.

Eagerly she took it to the Dwaraka Mai, and handed it over. To her utter consternation the lady (Durgabai) placed it last in the rows of food offerings. Baba, however, slowly moved to the back and picked up her dish and devoured the whole of it with great relish. This touched the lady to the bottom of her heart, and further strengthening her devotion in Baba.

*Leela 60:*  # Baba appears in the glass of alcohol as a warning

A devotee (name not mentioned) was once strolling in a shopping area of Girgaon, Mumbai. He saw a beautiful painting of Radha Krishna hung outside a shop called 'Akkalkot Fine Art Gallery'. Fascinated by that painting he stood for a long time to look at it. The shopkeeper asked him to step inside his shop, which he did. On the wall in front of him he saw a huge photograph of Baba. Assuming that the shopkeeper was also a devotee he asked the shopkeeper to tell him his experiences of Baba.

### Shantaram is cured of his addiction to alcohol
The shopkeeper, named Gondu Jaganath Naik, went to Shirdi in 1913, he then related his reason for that visit. "A friend of mine, named Shantaram, was addicted to alcohol, and it was ruining his

life. That friend went to Shirdi and sought refuge at Baba's feet. Although he had only 3 days leave, Baba made him stay for 6 days. Then Baba gave him *udi prasad* and he returned home.

"Needless to say he was cured of his addiction, and never touched alcohol in his life."

## The jeweller and his family visit Shirdi

Then he related another *leela*, "Here in Mumbai there is a jeweller, who is famous and affluent. I went to his home on one occasion, and he told me that he was very unhappy because his son was addicted to alcohol. Many a doctor had examined him and they said that alcohol would kill him prematurely. They had counselled the boy but the lad told them that death was welcome as he could not live even a day without alcohol." Naik at once remembered his friend, Shantaram, and advised the jeweller to go to Shirdi.

The jeweller along with his son and Naik went to Shirdi. During the journey the boy continued to drink. At Manmad the boy started vomiting incessantly. But as soon as they reached Shirdi the vomiting ceased. They had Baba's *darshan*, the father silently prayed for a cure and recovery of his son from alcoholism. Baba made them stay for 4 days, and the lad was detoxified of alcohol.

His progress was so quick that on their return journey when the father asked his son if he wanted a drink the lad refused. The same lad who would drink day and night, who had lost control, and would often be found lying here and there in a semiconscious state was now normal. The family was full of joy and wonder that such a malignant habit was got rid of so easily. The lad started gaining weight and his sallow complexion was lost, and he became cheerful again. It seemed that he was on the right path, and had control of his life.

## They offered alcohol as prasad and then ingested it

Their visit to Shirdi took place in *Vaishak* (the month of May and June as per the Hindu calendar.) Three months later, in the month of *Bhadrapad* (the month of September and October as per the Hindu calendar) was the festival of *Navrathri*. The family performed *Gowri puja*. On the completion of the 9 days of *puja,* there was much merriment and all the relatives were present.

It was a tradition with them that on the final day they all consumed a little alcohol as *prasad*. Thus they gave their son a glass of alcohol. He refused to consume it, so they forced him. They handed him a glass of alcohol, then the boy said, "I don't want it as I see Baba in it."

The relatives coerced him saying, "Take just a glass of the *prasad* or the family will incur the wrath of the goddess." So he gave up and drank glass after glass with abandonment. That night in a totally drunken state he went to bed. Then tragedy struck, some time at night while still in bed he lit a *bidi* (indigenous cigarette wrapped in a leaf), somehow the mattress caught on fire and the boy was fatally burned. Thus ended his life.

Ref: *Sai Leela Shake 1846. Ank 9 and 10. Year 5 (1928)*

## Leela 61:    Baba's udi saves the life of both mother and child

In *Shri Sai Satcharita*, the *leela* of the Jamner miracle is given. Baba sends his *udi*, along with *Adkars arati* to Nana Sahib Chandorkar. Ramgir Bua delivers it to him. At that crucial moment Mina Tai is in great pain, and is in danger of losing her life. Upon receiving the *udi*, her mother applies some of it on her forehead. And gives the rest as *udi tirth* to drink. Following this she has a safe delivery. A similar *leela* is given below.

A *Kayasth Prabhu* (a caste) from Mumbai, along with his wife came to Shirdi. (Unfortunately their names are not mentioned). They stayed at Shirdi for several months. His wife was pregnant, and was due to deliver any time. One night at 10 o'clock she went into labour. The pain was unbearable, and the mother soon became cold and clammy.

As Shirdi was a small village they could not take her to a hospital. Nor were there any nurses, or midwives. Two ladies from the neighbourhood came to attend to her. They realised that the baby was lying athwart; this frightened them out of their wits. The labour pains were coming on fast, and they felt they would lose both the mother and child.

One of the ladies took some *udi* and mixed it in water and gave it to her to drink. Then she earnestly prayed to Baba. Five minutes later the child was delivered, but he was quite blue as the umbilical cord was coiled around his neck. Finally, the baby started breathing normally, and the mother's life was saved. The father was extremely happy with the outcome because other eminent doctors in Mumbai had said that the delivery would be life-threatening for the mother and the child, so they sought refuge in Shirdi.

Ref: *Sai Leela Jyeshth Shake 1845. Ank 3. Year 1 (1923)*

## *Leela 62:* **Dr Talvalkar treats a fatal disease with udi and plain water**

Dr Talvalkar hailed from Amravati, and set up his practice in Indore. He first visited Shirdi in 1917, and since then he made frequent visits to have Baba's *darshan*. On one of his visits Baba gave him some *udi*, which he guarded with his life. He used the *udi* sparingly but wisely.

His medical practice flourished, by Baba's grace. Often the other doctors referred their patients to him, when they had difficulty in treating them. Dr Talvalkar's daily routine was like this; he would first do Baba's *puja*, and then go to his office to treat the patients.

Once a very serious patient was referred to him. He made a 'house call' and upon checking the patient he realised that the patient was at death's door. He comforted the relatives, and asked them to send some one to his clinic for the medication. The doctor returned home and stood in front of Baba's photograph. "Baba! man has tried all kinds of remedies and failed. Now, you are the only one who can save this patient," he said.

After praying to Baba, he wondered what his line of treatment would be. Suddenly it occurred to him that he should give the patient Baba's *udi*, and leave the rest to Baba. So he devised an ingenious plan. He took an empty medicine bottle and filled it with water; on the front of the bottle he stuck a dosage marker of three doses. Then he made three small packets of the *udi* and kept them on the medicine counter. When the relative came to collect the medicines, he said, "This medicine will definitely improve the patient's condition. You need to give him one packet, followed by a dose from the bottle every three hours. I want you to come in the evening and report the patient's condition."

That evening the relative did come, and told the doctor that the patient was feeling better already. Then Dr Talvalkar prescribed the regular medicines. Slowly, but steadily the patient regained his health. When he had fully recovered the patient came to the doctor's office. He paid the bill and gratefully added some more money. The doctor refused to accept it, saying, "I did not pull you out of the jaws of death. It was the grace of some one else who did that. I was just an instrument in his plan. It was his *udi* that worked for you. So you must visit Shirdi."

Some time later the doctor brought that patient to Shirdi. The grateful patient put a great deal of *dakshina* in the collection box. They did *puja*, and attended the *arati*. Then the doctor said, "This is Sai Baba, who gave you the second chance. My medicines did not cure you. It was his *udi tirth* and his grace that worked on you."

This true incident occurred in 1937. But the *udi* was given to the doctor in 1917 by Baba. Ref: *Nir Vaani cha Sakha*

# Leela 63:    Kavaji Patil does not heed
Baba's advice and disaster strikes

Kavaji Patil lived in Andheri, Mumbai. It was his earnest desire to build a temple in the memory of his late father. An acquaintance of his suggested that the idol of *Vani devi* be installed there. The two of them went and chose the idol, and everything was finalised.

Then he went to Shirdi, to seek Baba's advice. When he told Baba every detail, Baba said, "No, do not install a new idol, but reinstall the idols that your ancestors prayed to." Kavaji was full of doubt, as his acquaintance had convinced him about the new idol. So Kavaji repeatedly asked Baba the same question, and repeatedly Baba gave the same answer. He pestered Baba time and again. Finally Baba said, "I have repeatedly told you not to install a new idol, but to reinstall the idols your ancestors prayed to. Now do what you like, but you will have to bear the consequences."

Kavaji then returned home, and made all arrangements for the installation. The day his acquaintance arrived Plague broke out, and many people lost their lives. Seeing this the acquaintance ran away to his village, and this made Kavaji lose faith in his acquaintance. Then he himself decided to install an idol of another Goddess. Following the installation of the Goddess, Kavaji was plagued by many troubles and disasters. He became extremely sick and hovered at death's door. It was by Baba's grace that he recovered. After shedding many tears, his faith in Baba strengthened.

He went to Shirdi and laid his head on Baba's feet, but this time with faith and devotion. Again Baba said the same thing, "Install the idols your ancestors worshipped. And take away the idol that is currently there." This time Kavaji followed Baba's advice and he found peace and happiness. In gratitude he wrote a *bhajan* on Baba's divinity and compassion.

Ref: *Sai Leela Kartik Shake 1847. Ank 8. Year 6 (1925)*

## Leela 64: Baba makes Agul Karim Khan stay at Shirdi for 10 days

❝Baba with an open heart conversed with the common folks and watched the dancing and gesticulating of the *Muralis,* he also nodded appreciatively as he listened to the songs and *ghazals.* And yet his *samadhi* was unperturbed." (Ref: *Shri Sai Satcharita* Chapter 4, *Ovi* 49).

Often Baba would tie *ghungurus* (tiny bells) on his ankles and dance in ecstasy. Baba appreciated talent and responded to it from his heart. The *leela* given below is about the famous *Hindustani* classical singer, whom Baba kept in Shirdi for 10 days.

It was customary for any musician, singer or any talented person to present themselves in Baba's *durbar.* Baba loved music and had a great deal of knowledge of it. Agul Karim Khan was one such talented singer. He had graduated in *Hindustani* classical music from the *Kiranna Gharana.* This gifted singer had a voice that tinkled like a bell, besides being a wise man. His name and fame spread far and wide.

In 1914, Khan Sahib had a programme in Amalnere, where he was invited by Pratap Shet. There Shriman Butti and various other devotees attended his programme and invited him to Shirdi. Khan Sahib cancelled the rest of his programme to visit Shirdi. He had a great respect for saints and he felt this was a good opportunity to pay homage to Baba.

He and his entourage of students and musicians arrived in Shirdi. They camped in the hall of Kote Patil's house. In the evening when the usual *bhajans* took place in the Dwaraka Mai, Khan Sahib was sitting alongside the singers. Then Khan Sahib went for Baba's *darshan*. Baba blessed him and made inquiries about him. There Baba asked him to sing a *bhajan* in Marathi. In a melodious voice he sang, "हेचि दान देगा देवा…"

"God give me this boon that I never forget you." (Tukaram's *Abhang* in raga Pillo.) Baba enjoyed the *bhajan* so much that he closed his eyes and heard it with wrapped attention. Then Baba said, "You ask for a boon in such a way that one cannot but give it to you. Now don't make haste to leave Shirdi. Do not worry about your family, everything will be all right." Then turning to Kote Patil, Baba said, "Give them Shirdi's *badashai* treatment."

The next day Khan Sahib received a telegram from his wife (Taaharabai) that his daughter (Gulabkali) was seriously sick and he should return home. Khan Sahib brought the telegram and handed it to Baba. Baba reassured him and asked him to bring his family to Shirdi. His wife and daughter, came to Shirdi. Khan Sahib carried his daughter, who was hovering at death's door, and laid her on Baba's feet.

Baba took some ash from his *chillum* and mixed it with jaggery. Baba made a mixture of it with water, and gave it to her to drink. After two days of this treatment Gulabkali was on her feet. Baba kept Khan Sahib and his family in Shirdi for 10 days.

Meanwhile, Khan Sahib asked the other devotees, "What are the *bhajans* that Baba likes?" Then he learned them by heart and practised them, thus he was ready to present them before Baba.

The entourage of singers, students and musicians consisted of about 20 people. Taaharabai asked Mrs Kote Patil if she could do the cooking and household chores. Mrs Patil replied, "What you say is right, but I have orders from Baba to look after your comforts. You can however tell me what you would like to eat. And how you would like to eat and I shall prepare it the same way." That night Taaharabai sang some *bhajans* and ended with *Gaaliyan Lotangana* and Baba was very happy.

Khan Sahib was concerned about his music school at Poona, and Baba reassured him. Baba then gave him permission to leave, saying, "You are eager to go, but do not return to Poona. Go to Varahad, as the cotton trees are in full bloom." Then Khan Sahib sang some of the Baba's favourite *bhajans* and those that Baba particularly liked,

- जे का रंजले गांजले त्यासी म्हणजे जो आपुले

- इस तन धन की कौन बढाई, देखते नैनो में मिट्टी मिलाई

- and *Jogiya'*

Baba blessed him and stroked his back and gave him a silver coin, saying, "Do not spend this coin, keep it in your pocket at all times." Then he gave 5 rupees to Taaharabai and asked her to keep it in her trunk. Baba took a lot of *pedas* and put it in her *ooti*. 'Filling the *ooti*' is a wonderful tradition, especially in Maharashtra, where the elderly or the guru blesses and fills the *ooti*. Women usually keep their heads covered as a sign of respect. The lady gathers up that part of her sari that diagonally covers the abdomen and places both her hands beneath that part of the sari when she receives the blessing (i.e., coconut or whatever the guru may give). Here the *sadguru* Sai Baba put a large number of *pedas* in her *ooti*.

This was a blessing that any devotee of Baba would covet.

Ref: *Sai Sagar Deepavali Visesh Ank. September and October 2001*

## Leela 65: Ganpat Rao Bodas of the kirloskar natak mandali visits Shirdi

Ganpat Rao never liked sadhus or saints. So intense was his dislike that if any of his friends went to meet them, he would make fun of them. On one occasion he had to stay at Ahmednagar for a while. There he got an irresistible urge to visit Shirdi.

His friend Baala Sahib Mirkar was a *Mamlatdar* at Kopergaon. He contacted him and told him about his desire to visit Shirdi. On a Sunday they went to Shirdi.

They went to the Dwaraka Mai, and both of them prostrated at Baba's feet. Bodas offered a coconut and tobacco. Baba asked him for *dakshina*. Then Baba asked him to fill his *chillum* with the tobacco, which is an honour. Bodas placed a rupee in front of Baba as *dakshina*. In his own characteristic way Baba enquired about his well being. Then said, "If people fight amongst themselves what can one do." At that time Bodas had had a fight with his assistant. Then Baba asked him to stay for lunch.

He went to the *bhojanalaya* (dining hall) where some one asked him about the amount he would give as *dakshina*. Then the man said, "When Baba asks for *dakshina* you should empty your purse." Bodas liked the advice and decided to do just that. When it was time for him to leave he went to take Baba's permission. Baba readily gave him permission and asked him for *dakshina*. This time Bodas did not miss the opportunity and he happily emptied his purse before Baba. Baba blessed him, applied *udi* on his forehead and said, "Just as you have given me *dakshina*, Lord Narayan will give you an abundance of wealth."

After this visit to Shirdi, Bodas became famous as an actor, and with fame came wealth. He states that after his pilgrimage to Shirdi, he 'raked in money'. The *dakshina* that he gave Baba was returned in a millionfold. Ref: *Sai Sagar Deepavali Visesh Ank. September and October 2001*

## Leela 66: **Bai Sahib of Baroda visits Shirdi**

In the year 1904, Bai Sahib of the royal family came for Baba's *darshan*. The entourage consisted of Bai Sahib, the famous doctor from Mumbai Sir Firoz Shah Mehta, Sir Balchandra Batwadekar, and their staff.

They came with a lot of gifts. There was a huge platter of silver coins, and another platter heaped with guineas. They placed the gifts before Baba which he did not even glance at, let alone touch. Then he returned the gifts.

At that time Mhalsapathy was sitting with Baba, so they offered their gifts to him. Mhalsapathy, however, would not accept anything from anybody without first consulting Baba. Then Baba said, "*आपल्याला गिनीशी काय कर्तव्य? आपल्याला आपली गरिबीच चांगली ।।* "

"What have we to do with guineas? Our poverty is good for us." Thus the entourage returned without giving any gifts.

Ref: *Sai Sagar Deepavali Vishesh Ank. September and October issue 2001*

## Leela 67: **Some insights on Baba given by M B Rege**

In Rege's letter, dated 3rd September 1968, he states and I quote, "I shall now give brief replies to your questions. The first one was about his complexion. Baba had a wheatish complexion. But there was some brilliance which cannot be described. At times there would be a bright aura around his face. The second one was about Baba's height. His height was approximately 5'10". The third one was about Baba's daily routine. His daily routine was that in the morning just after sunrise he would wash his face and hands sitting in the verandah. Then he would be in his seat smoking tobacco (clay pipe) and people would come for *darshan*. About an hour later he would go to the Lendi. The route was through the village, and Radha Krishna Mai would sweep the road to the Lendi backwards so as not to step on the swept portion.

"The Lendi then was a sort of deep canal. Some people accompanied him while others waited for his return. He would be there for an hour. On his return he would wash his feet and then go out for *bhiksha*. During my visits I would accompany him. As far as I know he went to Lendi once a day.

The fourth one was his eating habit. I never saw Baba eating non-vegetarian food. But from 1911 to 1918 when the devotees prepared several dishes of food and sent the same as *naivedya,* he would not accept it and ate only the things he got from *bhiksha*. I cannot vouch for the correctness of the statement in *Satcharita*. He never took anything for breakfast as far as I know. His meal was only the afternoon lunch, after *arati*."

## Baba's aasan (seat)

Kaka Dixit states that at first the floor of the Dwaraka Mai was muddy and damp. Then tile flooring was laid. At that time it was winter and bitterly cold. As Baba did not accept change easily, so on the day that he slept in the *Chavdi* the work of laying the tiles was done. Dixit brought all the masons and workers from Mumbai. The whole night they worked in the light of an oil lamp. Stealthily they completed the task.

It was impossible to stand on the tiles for they were very cold. Baba would arise before dawn and come to the Dwaraka Mai. Then he would sit on his (sack) *aasan* in solitude. The considerate Dixit thought that Baba would feel the chill when he sat, so this is what he did. He placed a cotton mattress in Baba's sitting area, and over it he placed the sack that Baba used. Baba saw the mattress below and asked him to remove it, and thus sat on the sack.

As Baba would not accept the cotton mattress, immediately they set out and made a mattress of sack cloth. This Baba did not object to. That evening after his rounds Baba asked them to remove the mattress. So every evening Dixit would take the mattress to his *wada*, and return with it early next morning. So the sack mattress became Baba's *aasan*.     Ref: *Sai Leela Margashrish Shake 1857. Year 12 (1936)*

*Leela 68:* **Shyamrao Jayker's portrait of Baba in Dwaraka Mai**

This famous and beautiful portrait is a masterpiece and is widely known as 'the Dwaraka Mai pose'.

Traditionally, the mother is the care giver. When the father returns home after working all day, the child runs to him. The child who has been playing outside is covered with dust, and has a runny nose. The father will invariably call the mother to clean the child. The mother on the other hand is oblivious to the snort and dust, lovingly she holds her child close to her bosom, and cleans him. When the child is clean and has proper clothes on, the father says, "This child is mine."

With this analogy the Dwaraka Mai pose is interpreted. Baba sits next to the railing and his form is a triangle with the apex of the *bilva* leaf on it. It signifies 'Mount Meru', the abode of mother Parvati. So he is the Mother calling her children (us) to come and take refuge in him. The *Kakad arati* says, "*Tu shanti ksmeca meru ho. Tu bhavarnavice taru guruvara*" (You are the mountain Meru of peace and forgiveness. You are the bark that ferries us across this mundane existence.)

His left hand rests on the railing and all the fingers are visible. Each finger is a sort of *mudra* which could mean – 1. The three *Gunas*, i.e., *Rajo*, *Tama* and *Satva*. 2. The three *Shariras*, i.e., *Stoola*,

*Shukshma* and *Karana*. 3. The *Indryias* with *Arshidvargas*. 4. The five *Pranas*, i.e., *Prana, Apana, Udana, Samana* and *Vyana*. 5. The five *koshas*, i.e., the five sheaths are *Annamaya kosha, Pranamaya kosha, Manomaya kosha, Vigyanamaya kosha* and *Anandmaya kosha*.

The middle, ring and little finger of the left hand are turned in, and represent *manas, budhi* and *chitta*. These are inside every *jeev atma*. While the index finger is out and pointing down, this could represent *aham* (pride and ego). This could also represent 'the compassionate mother' saying, "Come with all your faults, pride of earthly possessions and ego, my lap is always there to rock you my child." The right leg is bent at the knee so the child can lie there. The left leg is firmly planted on the ground representing firmness of resolve. Baba saying, "I am firm in my promise to accept you, and if you take one step I will take ten steps towards you."

The thumb which represents the *parabrahma* is turned in pointing to himself. It's the *sadguru* or *parabrahma* who can cleanse the *jeev atma* of all these impurities, and undesirable traits. This could be the representation of this beautiful portrait.

## Leela 69: Dr Keshev B Gavankar gives interesting insights on Baba

Volumes have been written about Baba's divinity and *leelas*, but Baba lived in Shirdi as a Fakir. He had endearing human qualities of playing pranks, dancing, singing and joking. This made him readily accessible to his devotees, whether rustic villagers or lawyers. Some of these endearing qualities are given below.

### Baba laughed heartily, and played pranks
When Tatya, Mhalsapathy and Baba slept in the Dwaraka Mai, Baba would get up and put Mhalsapathy's feet on Tatya's chest or vice

versa. When they awoke and saw this, they would ask Baba, "Baba, who did this?" To which Baba would laugh heartily.

## Body Massage

Whenever Baba perceived a devotee was leaning towards the pride of bodily strength, Baba asked that devotee to massage his body. Some of these devotees were Bhayaji Kote, Shama, Tatya Kote, Madhu Fasle, Anna Chinchinaker, Mausibai and Durgabai. Baba made them massage his body till they were drenched in perspiration. When they had no more strength to lift their hand, only then would he ask them to stop. Some times he asked two of them to massage him.

Baba often caused fights between the devotees, take Shama and the *Ramdasi* for instance. Baba told the *Ramdasi* a lie, that his stomach ached, and sent him to get some medicine. When he was away Baba took his 'Vishnushasranam' (book) and gave it to Shama. When the *Ramdasi* returned, he fought with Shama for the book.

Mausibai and Anna Chinchinaker were massaging Baba at the same time and when they came in close proximity to each other, Baba said that Anna wanted to kiss Mausibai, thus causing a fight between them.

## Tatya Kote Patil and Baba's relationship

The *rinanubandhic* ties between Baba and Tatya Kote Patil were deep and unfathomable.

In *Shri Sai Satcharita* Chapter 42, *Ovi* 65 and 68, it is stated that 'Baba gave up his life for Tatya'. While Tatya recovered from his fatal illness, Baba took *niryan*, i.e., left this world.

However, their relationship was more like friends or sibling. They played, ate and slept together. Some of their interactions are given below.

In the summer it would get extremely hot. Baba would make Tatya sleep in front of the blazing *dhuni*. After he was sound asleep, Baba would cover him with his blanket. Drenched in perspiration Tatya would wake up, wipe off the perspiration and inquire how this happened? Baba responded with peals of laughter.

Baba would tickle Tatya off and on. Tatya would ask him why he did this, and Baba laughed.

Often Baba hid Tatya's *uparna* (shawl) behind the pillar in the Dwaraka Mai. Then Baba pushed and shoved him behind the pillar. At other times Baba placed his fingers over both his eyes so as to blindfold him. This was followed by peals of laughter with 'child like innocence'.

Shirdi was a small and remote village without playgrounds. Bhayaji Appa and Madhu Fasle would come to the Dwaraka Mai and play with stones. Baba would stand close by and distract them. Slowly and stealthily he would keep his foot on one of the stones, and hide it. When they found a stone missing they would ask Baba whether he took it. Innocently Baba would say, "No *re*." After the players entreated him to return the stone; Baba would slowly put the stone back in its place. This prank always made him laugh.

Often Baba played *fugadi* (a game in which two people cross their forearms then clasp the other person's hand and go round and round).

## Songate or the game of chess

Sometimes Baba played chess with Tatya. On the nights that Baba slept in the *Chavdi*, the villagers gathered and played chess. Radha Krishna Mai along with Baba's requirement for the night (i.e., tumbler of water) would send the 'chess board' and then they would play far into the night. Often they were heard shouting and fighting.

From *Dnayneshwari* (Chapter 11, Verse 548) this line has been taken. "Many times I had wrestling matches with you. While playing the game of dice, I spoke to you rudely and even fought with you" ('You' is referred to Shama and Tatya). Arjun and Krishna also had contests in wrestling and playing the game of dice.

## Wrestling matches

In *Shri Sai Satcharita* the *leela* of the wrestling match between Baba and Mohiddin Tamboli is given. Baba loses the match, and it becomes a milestone which changes his lifestyle. From that time Baba started wearing *kafnis* and adopted the life of fakiri.

Baba liked to wrestle; he encouraged wrestlers and gave them prizes when they wrestled well. Tatya knew this and they would wrestle sometimes. Tatya would put his hand under Baba's buttocks, and lift him. "*Arre* Kothya (a nick name), I will fall. Be careful or you may sprain a muscle," cautioned Baba. Though no such thing ever happened.

Baba often massaged Tatya's body. When Tatya was relaxed, Baba would swiftly prostrate at his feet. Holding Baba's hands, Tatya would plead with Baba not to do such a thing, for it was not right. In reply Baba said, "Hush Kothya, what do you know."

At other times Baba held Tatya's hands and did namaskar to him. Then he said, "Jai Dev, Jai Dev." Embarrassed, Tatya, complained to Baba and ask him not to repeat that again. Encouraged by Tatya's embarrassment, Baba saluted him and said, "*Aleyukum Salaam!*"

## Baba looks at himself in the mirror

Tatya took liberties with Baba, who seemed to enjoy it. Tatya often removed Baba's *shirvesh* (head dress) and placed his *Schinde Shai Pagdi* (turban worn by people of his caste) on Baba's head. Then he placed his *uparna* (shawl covering the shoulder) on Baba's shoulders. Tatya got a mirror and handed it to Baba. Like an ordinary human being, Baba preened and made appreciative gestures.

Baba shrugged his shoulders, repeatedly blinked his eyes, in wonder. "Kothya, don't I look like this all the time? Isn't my lifestyle like this," said Baba. A while later Baba removed Tatya's turban and shawl, and wore his *kafni* and *koupin*.

Tatya and Baba had *panga* or arm wrestling competitions. Baba would use his right hand, while Tatya had to use his left hand. Baba gently pressed Tatya's fingers, then a little harder. Tatya not to be outdone, reciprocated by pressing even harder, and harder. Suddenly Baba cried out, "*Arre* Kothya, are you trying to fracture my fingers?" This was followed by peals of laughter.

## Baba dances in the Dwaraka Mai

Sometimes in the afternoon between 4 and 5 p.m., Baba danced in the Dwaraka Mai. The dance was full of exaggerated movements.

He bent his legs, hands and neck in strange ways, and rolled his eyes about. At other times he stuck his tongue out. Often he joked and laughed merrily.

Like Lord Shri Krishna, he danced on one foot and the toes of the other foot. This was exclusively for Tatya, and if any body entered the Dwaraka Mai he became calm and serene.

Tatya and Baba hopped about like small children. They played in abandon.

## Baba calls his devotees by pet names

The Dwaraka Mai was Baba's whole *samsar*, the devotees came there for his *darshan*. Some came for health, wealth or progeny. Others came to behold his divinity.

Baba had an endearing way of calling them by pet names. They are given below; unfortunately I can't identify all of them but you may be able to.

They are Kaasha, Appa, Shyamia (Madhavrao Deshpande), Goodmukhea, Baburao, Vaman, Kondaji, Andaji, Dada (Kelkar), Mama Shipurda, Langda Kaka (Dixit), Mota Kaka, Pradhan, Ganu (Das Ganu), Anna, Hemand (Dabolkar).

The other names were Bhau, Dadiwala, Takki (Sagunmeru), Hallalkhor (Abdulla), Veda master, Bodka Brahmin, Ghode doctor, Bhattyacha karta, Bammanache porta, Bade Baba, Bapu Sahib (Jog), Taapu Sahib, Ardha Kholhati, Mahadya Padhya, Aardha Gandu, Butya, Avdaasa, Ram Krishni, Radha Krishni (the last three names were for Radha Krishna Mai).

Mavsi, Durgi, Hedambi (Mrs Chinikar), Radha Maami, Byja Maami, Sai Aayi, Taai Aayi, Bhima Bai, Soni Bai, Pillay, Nanda, Fanda, Chindi Chor (Dev), Baalbodka, Buttiche Javai and Dhabaji Ganpat Rao.

Each of these devotees had a specific job to do, and they had to perform it. One could not do the other person's job, and this was sort of a law.

Lord Krishna is also said to have called the *gopis* by names other than their own.

## Some devotees respond to Baba's human form

Because Baba behaved like an ordinary human being, a few of the devotees argued with him, and often spoke irreverentially to him.

After Baba's *mahasamadhi* Shama would remember how he behaved and talked to Baba, and cry bitterly. He told Dr Gavankar this, "I thought Baba was an ordinary human being like me. I did not recognise the divinity and spiritual wealth in him, so I behaved rudely.

"I joked and made fun of him, and said '*Tu* and *re*'. Often I got angry with him and fought raising my voice, but worst of all I insulted him by calling him a liar, beggar and a thief. I used many insulting and derogatory words without realizing that I was talking to god and *parabrahma*." While many people from far-off places came and rolled in the dust of his feet, I being so near really did not recognise your divinity, hence I insulted you. Nonetheless my wrong doing is so vast that even the three *loks* are small compared to it. Nevertheless you loved and cuddled me like a child. Now that all this is in the past, what is the remedy?

"This world will never again witness such an omnipresent, omnipotent, omniscient and compassionate god, like my *Deva*, who walked, talked and laughed like a human being."

Then Shama cried inconsolably.

When Baala Shimpi went to his village, he came to the Dwaraka Mai and asked Baba for a kiss, then Baba kissed him on his cheek and sent him home.            Ref: *Shirdi che Sai Baba by Dr K B Gavankar*

Many comparisons are made between Baba and Lord Krishna, here are some of them. Lord Krishna got the name of Govardan Giri because he held the mountain with his little finger. Thus a canopy was formed where the devotees took shelter, during the rain storm.

In Shirdi the villagers ran to the Dwaraka Mai with their cattle and took shelter under its roof. Baba then went to the edge of the *otta* and shouted at the rain to stop. Though the other gods and goddesses of Shirdi could not help, Baba did. Even *Varun*, the Lord of the rains, obeyed Baba's orders. The storm with all its fury abated and stopped.            Ref: *Shri Sai Satcharita Chapter 11*

Krishna used to play his flute standing on a rock, while Baba sat on the rock (the stone). Vitthal stood on a brick and Baba slept with the brick under his head.

Both wandered in the forest, Bayaja Ma used to go and search for Baba and feed him. This was in the early days. Later when Baba came to stay in the Dwaraka Mai, he would still go to the forest. This made the villagers think he was a mad fakir.

## Leela 70: Raghuvir Bhaskar Purandhare

Purandhare worked as a clerk in the Department of Railway. He was not affluent, and had a large family to take care of. His faith in Baba was immense and unshakable. After his first meeting with Baba, he laid his *tan, man, dhan* (total surrender) at Baba's feet.

### Mrs Purandhare delivers a child with difficulty

The year was 1916 and the month was October, when Mrs Purandhare, went to her parents home. There she delivered a baby boy. Though the baby seemed healthy, he had a thick growth of hair all over his body. His nose was very large and crooked. The baby was only 14 days old, but the mother decided to return home with her child.

Her parents repeatedly asked her not to go home just yet, as she was quite unwell. Post-delivery she had swelling of her feet and there were signs of eclampsia (Post-delivery convulsions). Not heeding their advice she returned home and the next day she was extremely ill.

Dr Khadwale examined her, and felt that her condition was serious. He advised her to get admitted in his hospital. Purandhare did not heed his advice, and asked the doctor to treat her at home. Dabolkar and Joshi came to visit them that evening. When they saw the condition of his wife, they were mortified and asked Purandhare to take her to the hospital at once. Purandhare had full faith in Baba and replied, "If Baba wishes to save her, she will be saved here only without any treatment. If she is not to be saved, admission in the hospital will be futile." Nonetheless Joshi insisted and coerced him to take her to the hospital. Finally, Purandhare agreed and it was decided that they would take her in the morning.

## Baba cures Mrs Purandhare with udi

Purandhare had reluctantly agreed to take his wife to the hospital the next day. That night around midnight, Baba cured her.

Baba entered his home through the closed door. He appeared in his usual *roopa* clad in his *kafni*, a *jholi* hung from his shoulder with the *satka* in his hand. Baba had the look of Narasimha, and was extremely angry. Baba took his *satka* and made a threatening gesture as if to beat Purandhare. He was shouting fowl abuses at some unseen object.

Then he strode to where Mrs Purandhare lay and applied hot *udi* on her forehead. When this occurred Mrs Purandhare screamed, "Baba has applied hot *udi* on my forehead, hence it is burning. My whole body is burning. Look Baba is standing next to my pillow. Now I will recover, and I won't die. There is no need to be anxious." The next day Dabolkar and Joshi arrived to take her to the hospital. Purandhare told them about the *leela* of the previous night. Dabolkar was reluctant to believe it. Joshi was calm, and believed every word of it.

The child was hardly two weeks old, when his mother had recovered fully. She was eager to take her child to Shirdi, and place him at Baba's feet. Ref: *Shirdi che Sai Baba by Dr K B Gavankar*

## He has finally found me

When his son was about 7 months old, Purandhare and his family visited Shirdi. Baba picked up the child and laid him on his lap. Patting the child, he said, "This Bhau has been searching for me, for a very long time. Now he has finally found me." Then both of them (Baba and the child) held their respective abdomens and laughed merrily.

Purandhare's son was born under the influence of *mool nakshatra* (an inauspicious birth sign). This is considered very unfortunate for the parents. His friends and relatives advised him to perform *shanti havan* (*puja* to appease the star) but Purandhare was reluctant to do so. The devotees at Shirdi also advised him to perform the *shanti havan*.

One day Anna Chinchinaker told Baba about it. He told Baba that Purandhare was obstinate, and refused to perform the *shanti puja*. "आपण मी असतांना त्याने काय म्हणून शांती करावी । । त्याला जिकडे तिकडे साई मौला दिसतो । । तो वेडा आहे असो गरीबोका वाली अल्ला है । ।"

"Anna, when I am here to look after his welfare, then for what reason will he do *shanti puja*. He sees Sai *Moulla* here, there and everywhere, Anna. And he has become mad with love and devotion. What can I say to such a person? Let it be so. Allah is the saviour of the poor."

Purandhare's god was Sai, and his faith in him was deep and unshakable. Ref: *Shirdi che Sai Baba by Dr K B Gavankar*

## Purandhare pines for Baba's darshan

During the Christmas vacation Purandhare decided to accompany his family to his hometown. There both the mother and child could relax. They would be looked after by the relatives and the mother would not have to do the household chores, thus she could bond with the baby.

On the day of their departure they were to board the train at Bandra station. Purandhare purchased the tickets, and the train was due in 20 minutes. While they waited, Purandhare had an irresistible urge to go to Shirdi and have *darshan* of Baba. As the minutes ticked away the urge became stronger. He told his mother about it, his mother told him to drop them off at home and then go to Shirdi.

The train finally arrived and they boarded it, but by then Purandhare had decided to go to Shirdi and not his hometown. Purandhare told his family, "You proceed and go home, but I will continue my journey in this very train and go to Shirdi." He made all the necessary arrangements for their journey and went to Shirdi.

Purandhare got off at Kopergaon and got a *tonga* to Shirdi. He found a *tonga* at once and the *tongawalla*, Hassan, informed him that both Baba and Radha Krishna Mai were very ill. It was about 9 a.m., when he reached Shirdi. He went straight to the Dwaraka Mai, there Baba was surrounded by many devotees as every one was concerned about his health.

Purandhare went into the sanctum sanctorum, where Baba said, "Bhau, you have come at last. For the past 3 or 4 days I have been awaiting your arrival. Don't leave me, but go to Ram Krishni now and stay there. Don't go here and there."

Purandhare was filled with anguish to see Baba's condition. Baba had stopped eating, but there was no change in his daily routine. He went for his *bhiksha* rounds, and to Lendi Baugh with the help of three to four devotees. Purandhare was extremely saddened by the condition of Baba's health; he had lost weight and was very weak.

One day Purandhare told Baba, "Baba, I will carry you when you go to Lendi Baugh and for *bhiksha*." Purandhare could not control himself and started sobbing. Baba pacified him, saying, "Don't cry. I will be all right in 4 days. Allah has given me this illness and it has to be borne by me. So don't cry. Why should you cry? Some days are good while other days are not. Why should you fear?"

Ref: *Shirdi che Sai Baba by Dr K B Gavankar*

## Purandhare is concerned about Mai's illness

Purandhare asked Baba about the medicines to be given to Mai. Baba told him that she would recover in two days. The next day, early in the morning Purandhare came running to Baba, and told him, "Mai is just not getting up, she is groggy and weak. Her condition is deteriorating. Give me some medicine for her. I will not leave until you do so."

Then Baba told him a remedy, and explained how to prepare and administer it.

Baba cures Radha Krishna Mai and how?

In *Shri Sai Satcharita* the *leela* of Baba climbing on the roof of Vamanrao Gondkar's house is given. Some more details are also added.

That afternoon Baba got a ladder and he placed it against the wall of Gondkar's house, and climbed up. He crossed the roof of Mai's house and wanted to descend from the other side, i.e., Narayan Teli's house. This was a miracle in itself. Baba was so weak that he needed two or three people to help him walk or be seated. Yet he got atop the roof without anybody's aide. By then the devotees had gathered below to see this. Tatya Patil was also amongst them.

Baba called out to him and asked him to help him get down. Tatya asked what he would give in return for this. Baba replied, "10 rupees. I climbed up here because I panicked; I felt that a whole lot of people were threatening to beat me." After this episode Radha Krishna Mai recovered.          Ref: *Shirdi che Sai Baba by Dr K B Gavankar*

## Leela 71:          Baba's 'rahem nazar' breathes life into a dead man

Das Ganu, a police constable, turned into a *kirtankar* by Baba's grace. Chapter 15 of *Shri Sai Satcharita* describes how Das Ganu was established in the *Naradeeya Kirtan Paddhati*. Baba admonished Das Ganu for his elaborate dress and outward show. The only prerequisite was purity of heart and soul with intense passion for *bhakti*.

Das Ganu had a wonderful metallic tinkling voice, and because of his *kirtans* Baba's fame spread throughout Maharashtra. He had a ritual that he followed, first he would take Baba's permission, then at the place of *kirtan* he would keep Baba's photograph on a stool, offer prayers to it then only would he start his *kirtan*.

On one of his visits to Shirdi, Das Ganu was invited to a village nearby. He went to take permission, when Baba said, "Ganya (Baba called Ganu, Ganya) take Bhau with you." Baba called Jyotindra Tarkhad 'Bhau'. Das Ganu had no problem in taking Bhau with him, but he did not want to break his routine with Baba. Bhau used to light petromax lanterns in the Dwaraka Mai daily and do Baba's *seva*. However, Baba told Ganu not to worry about that as some one else would light the lanterns. Baba insisted, rather ordered him, to take Bhau along with him.

The village was about 8 to 9 kilometres from Shirdi. They had to walk to the village due to lack of transportation. Finally they reached there and it was past dusk, and getting dark. They hung lanterns in the four corners of the place, then Das Ganu placed Baba's photograph on the stool, did *puja* and started the *kirtans*.

## The bhil leader challenges Baba to resurrect the dead person

A huge crowd that had gathered there were immersed in the *kirtan*. Then there was a commotion; about eight well-built *bhils* came there. They were carrying a dead body on a bier. The leader of the group came up to Das Ganu in a threatening stance and asked him to stop all the noise. Then he pointed to Baba's photograph and asked, "Who is this?" Das Ganu oblivious of what had happened waxed forth on the divinity and greatness of Baba. The leader then said, "If your God is so great he can surely give life to the dead?" The leader further threatened to kill all of them if the person was not resurrected.

Das Gunu politely asked them to be seated. Then he turned to Bhau and asked him his opinion. Bhau told Das Ganu to continue with the *kirtan* for he knew it was Baba's *leela*. Then he added, "Ganu Maharaj sing, *Sai rehem nazar karna bacchon ka palan karna* (Sai with your compassionate glance take care and look after your children.)" Then he added, "Leave the rest at Baba's feet. He will surely protect us." Das Ganu again started singing and soon he was immersed in it, oblivious of his surroundings he was dancing with joy and devotion. Bhau was looking intently at the dead person. After some time the dead person struggled and set himself free from the bier and sat up.

Bhau then went to Das Ganu and said, "Maharaj, stop the *kirtan* for a while. Baba has done our work. That man is alive. Now there is no danger to our lives." The leader and the group came to Das

112

Ganu and asked him about Baba. Then he promised Ganu that he and his relatives would definitely visit Shirdi.

After the incident Bhau and Das Ganu went to the Dwaraka Mai and fell at Baba's feet. Baba said, "*Arre* Ganya, if my Bhau had not accompanied you yesterday, you know what would have happened to you." Simultaneously they both replied, "Baba all this was your *leela*. Nevertheless please look after us and save us from these adverse situations, and continue to shower your blessings on us."

Ref: *Shri Sai Swanubhav Tarkhadanche*

## Leela 72: Shri Sai Baba Mandir Trust – Kohrale

Adam Jan Pathan was the grandson of Abdul Jan Pathan. Abdul came to Shirdi, and Baba asked him to go and live in Kohrale. His descendants still live there.

Adam had an intense desire to build a temple in the memory of his grandfather. So he put his proposition before the village panchayat. They approved it and gave him a parcel of land. Kohrale is a barren and rocky terrain. There is no water there and the lake had dried up. The task of levelling the land and building a structure on it was quite formidable.

Many youngsters in Kohrale pitched in and worked day and night, as Adam wanted to celebrate *Gurupurnima* there. *Gurupurnima* was 3 days away; nonetheless they built a mud hut. Then they plastered the interior with cement. While the work was in progress, the *parayan* of *Shri Sai Satcharita* was going on. In the end, this mud hut became the main temple.

Then Sada got involved, and a few rules were laid down. Donation in cash and kind were accepted with gratitude, but no one in the trust can ask, seek or beg for donations. If donations were given, the name of the donor would not be written on a plaque, or on the object donated. Sada felt that Baba was the donor and receiver. And no one can donate anything without Baba's consent.

## How Baba's padukas came to be enshrined there

In 1998 when I was collecting material for 'Ambrosia in Shirdi', I read somewhere that there were *padukas* of Baba at some place near Narsimha lodge. This fact was confirmed by Amrut Rao Gondkar (grandson of Vaman Rao Gondkar). Baba used to take *bhiksha* from this house.

Sada and I searched for the *padukas* but the area was full of rubble. One day as we were returning from the Dwaraka Mai, Sada pointed to the wall of the lodge and said, "This must be the *padukas*, as the structure above looks like a temple." I was aghast to hear this, as it was at ground level and embedded in the wall of the lodge.

Nonetheless we removed the rubble and there were the *padukas*. So we did some *puja* with incense sticks. The owner of the lodge provided some lighting, and the nearby shopkeepers lit incense sticks.

## The widening of the Palkhi road

On the 6th of May 2004, the Shirdi Sai Baba *Sansthan* set about widening the 'Palki road'. The front portion of Narsimha lodge was slated to be broken. In that portion the *padukas* were partly embedded in the wall. We were very concerned lest they be damaged or broken. We had asked the *vidvan* (pundit) what had to be done if such a disaster occurred.

For three days we stood nearby waiting and watching. Finally the bulldozers came and tore down the wall. A ton of bricks fell on the *padukas*. That evening Adam and I were standing close by. What followed left me speechless. Three young men, who were the descendants of Shakaram Shielke, came over to us and handed over the *padukas*.

We got a van and took them to Kohrale. We did *abhishek* to the *padukas* and thenceforth daily *puja* was performed. Now we had to build a temple, as we couldn't keep the *padukas* lying there. We had to do *pran prathista*, so we decided to build a proper temple and thus fixed the a *muhurat* for *Gurupurnima*. *Gurupurnima* was three months away. Day and night the work was being done, and on *Gurupurnima* 2004, Baba came to the temple in the form of his *padukas*.

The *padukas* are over a hundred years old. Unlike most *padukas* they are not raised, but etched on the stone. It looks as if Baba stood on the stone and the sculptor etched the contours of his feet on that stone. They are the original *padukas* of Baba. In front of the *padukas*, there is a small hollow structure. It's said that Baba during his *bhiksha* rounds stood there and fed the birds, crows and dogs from the food collected. He then poured the liquid collected in that hollow cup. Sometimes he poured water in it so that the birds could drink it.

The temple is about 10 kilometres from Shirdi. There transportation is not readily available, so one had to go in his own vehicle or hire a vehicle on a 'to and fro' basis.

*Leela 73:*  # Madhavnath Maharaj

Lakshman alias Bhau Sahib Pradhan was working as a sub registrar. He went to meet Madhavnath Maharaj at the Chitra Koot *Sansthan*. Madhavnath, however, sent Pradhan to Shirdi with a message for Baba. The message was 'Tell Baba that he has not spoken directly to me about the present.'

Baba was seated in the Dwaraka Mai with his devotees, when he said, "Nath's son has come, we must prepare a feast for him and look after his comforts." The devotees seated there knew Baba spoke in riddles and parables so they waited, for the events to unfold. Just then Pradhan walked into the Dwaraka Mai. He gave Baba the message that Madhavnath had sent through him. Baba made him sit near him and said, "I had many sacks laden with gold on the donkey's back. On the way thieves stole the gold. For this reason it is very difficult to live in the neighbourhood of thieves. To teach you this, my brother has sent you to me. Today we will have Nath's *prasad*."

Then Pradhan was given a meal, and Baba made him sit next to him. When Pradhan asked for his permission to leave, Baba said, "Tell my brother that it's very difficult to live in this bad world. This is the *updesh* that was given to me by Baba." Pradhan carefully listened to everything Baba said, and then went back to Madhavnath's *Sansthan*.

### The possible meaning
The 'I' is *parabrahma*. The 'sacks of gold' represent the knowledge embedded within one's self. The 'donkey' represents people like us who carry the weight of this materialistic world on our backs. As we lead our lives, along the way thieves steal the gold or knowledge. The 'thieves' are maya and the *arshidvargas* combined together. They steal that knowledge, so it becomes difficult to strike a balance between *maya* and spiritual *sadhana*.        Ref: *Shirdi che Sai Baba by Dr K B Gavankar*

*Leela 74:*        **The packet of udi turns into bhukka of Pandharpur**

A devotee named Shankar Rao, accompanied his mother on a pilgrimage to Pandharpur. His mother was very eager to go have Vitthal's *darshan*. As Shirdi was on the way they decided to have Baba's *darshan* and then proceed.

They went to the Dwaraka Mai, prostrated before Baba and sat down. Baba said, "Go home", and gave the mother a packet of *udi*. The mother was disappointed, and she consoled herself thinking 'Shirdi is also Pandharpur'.

Upon reaching home she took out the packet of *udi*, and to her utter surprise, it was a packet of sweet smelling *bhukka* (black powder) from Pandharpur. She showed it to Shankar Rao, who said, "You really made a pilgrimage to Pandharpur so Baba gave you the *bhukka*."

Ref: *Sai Leela Margshrish Shake 1857. Ank 6. Year 12 (1935)*

*Leela 75:* # Mahali loved Baba passionately

Ravu was her maiden name, but her in-laws called her Radhe. While Baba called her Mahali.

She came to Shirdi after visiting almost every *dharmik shretra* (holy place of pilgrimage). Jejuri, Pandharpur, Alandi, Nevasa and Changdev, were some of the numerous places that she had visited. She came to Shirdi and stayed on because of her intense love and devotion for Baba.

When she was but a child she was married to Namdev Abha Savanth. However, she never lived with her husband, and was a celibate. Hence she had no children, or any relatives who could take care of her. She hailed from a small village in Sangamner called Khasarvadi. A Maratha by caste, she was about 75 years old.

The villagers thought she was mad because of her odd behaviour and mode of dressing. She was rather short and stout, and walked with the help of a stick. Her hair was uncombed, loose and matted. Illiterate, she talked continuously and irrelevantly. Mahali tied two pieces of rags around her feet. With a smile on her face, often she laughed for no apparent reason. She sat wherever she wanted and often lay on the ground or the road on her back. She addressed every male she met as 'Baba' and every female, as 'Aayi'.

## Mahali begs and blesses her benefactors
Mahali survived on the alms given by the numerous devotees that flocked to Shirdi. One could often hear her say, "Baba (a male

benefactor) feed me, I am hungry. Start giving me wages. Look after my welfare." Then she would bless him, with the same blessing every time. "You will remain a married couple all your life. You will have 5 grandsons. You will be happy, and my 'Shai Baba' (she called Baba, 'Shai Baba') will bless you. Give me clothes. Start giving me wages, O.K." This she said time and again. It was Baba who gave her food and clothing.

There was scarcity of water in Shirdi before the 'Godavari Canal Project' came into existence. Thus there were no gardens, or flowers readily available. Nonetheless, Mahali would go to the forest, pick wild flowers and offer them to her 'Shai Baba'. Some times she made garlands, and brought them for Baba. Baba gladly accepted her garlands, and would keep her garland around his neck the whole day. At other times she would pick fruits from the forest and offer them as *prasad* to Baba. Baba happily accepted those fruits because of her intense love and devotion.

## Baba accepts her innocent love and devotion
Baba would call out to her and give her food from his *bhiksha*.

One day Baba gave her a dream vision, and Mahali told everyone about it. "Baba came and kissed my cheek and said, 'त्यांनी माझे मुक्त घेतला म्हणाले, म्हाले तुझे मी कल्याण करीन, तुला एक बोट देईन, तुझा जे कोणी राग करतील, त्याच्या जवळ मी राहणार नाहीत ।। म्हळे तुला मी दागीने देईन, रुपया, दोन रुपये, पाच रुपये, रोज पर्यंत देईन. व तुझ्या जवळ राहीन ।।'

'Mahali, I will bless you with spiritual upliftment. I will give you one finger. Whoever is angry with you, I do not associate with him. Mahali, I will give jewellery and money. One rupee, two rupees, five rupees I will give henceforth, and I will stay with you.' Then he stood in front of me and said, 'Keep calling me Shai Baba Shai Baba, at all times, both day and night.'"

## The meaning of the dream is complicated
Baba used the word *kalyan* (bless you). He told her the secret or mystique of *prem bhakti*, i.e., devotion that has no boundaries, no motives and no expectations. Devotion filled with love, and the thought of the beloved deity (Baba) does not cease for even a

moment, be it day or night. In Mahali's case the name of her 'Shai Baba' was constantly on her lips.

I will give you jewellery or paisa (money), i.e., *punnya*. Merit of good karma must be accumulated as this is the real jewel.

One rupee is *adwaita*. The *jeev* has come solely from one, from Shiva, from *satya* or truth or from Sai.

Two rupees is *dwaita*. Shiva for his pleasure created *purush* and *prakruti*. The *vasana* became *prakruti* and *aham* became *purush*.

Five rupees is *panchtatva*, i.e., *panch mahabuth*. The human body is *panch mahabuth*.

'Shai Baba, Shai Baba' or *naam jaap*, was the only thing that Mahali knew. Incessantly she took Baba's name without even realizing that she was doing *naam jaap*. Was it little wonder that Baba blessed her?

One should do *naam jaap* with faith, love and devotion. By continuous *naam jaap* the gross body with all its *indryias* will be drawn towards the *jaap*. The *aham* will be controlled. *Adwaita* will remain and with it the feeling of 'you and me' will fade away. The *shadripu* like anger and jealousy will be controlled. Then knowledge or *atma jnana* is attained.

This devout lady, was thought to be mad, because of her outward appearance, but in fact she was a saint.

Ref: *Surdi che Sai Baba by Dr K B Gavankar*

# Bodha Paddhati

The meaning *bodha* is instruction or perception and *paddhati* means protocol or steps of a ritual.

This section of the book is called *bodha paddhati* or spiritual teachings of Baba. This is not the exact meaning of *bodha paddhati* but it conveys, what will follow.

Baba had a unique and delightful way of imparting *jnana* or knowledge. Sometimes he sent a devotee to an illiterate person, at other times he sent the devotee to get *dakshina* of a specific amount from another devotee. That specific amount carried a deeper meaning. Some *leelas* and teachings are given below.

Baba often taught in parables, he told *gohstis* or stories. They were told when his devotees were seated with him, but were meant for a certain devotee who was present there. Ganesh Shrikrishna Khaparde, in his book titled *Shirdi Diary*, has jotted down these parables. Unfortunately he has not given their meaning. Although, time and again he says Baba gave him yogic glances and he got the answers to his questions.

M B Rege told Baba, "If you want me to understand anything, then please don't talk to me in parables." Rege was intelligent, and highly educated, utterly spiritual, and had studied the *puranas* and other religious books.

If he found it hard to decipher what Baba said, then how can a fool like me understand anything? Undaunted, I have sought the help of my *spiritual guru* and tried to unravel the wisdom hidden there in.

The second part of this section contains the stories and his teachings through some parables.

## *Leela 76:* **Baba chi Vaishvadev chi shikvan**

### (Baba teaches appeasement of Vaishvadev or agni or fire)

On 28-07-1935, Baal Krishna V Dev went to Shirdi. He was seated in the Dwaraka Mai, when he saw Sagunmeru Naik perform *Vaishvadev puja*. Dev asked him about it and Sagunmeru replied, "I came to Shirdi around 1912, at that time I was jobless, nor did I have any business of my own. About six months later I started taking *naivedya* for Baba.

"About two years later, I had a dream where I was standing near the *dhuni*, when Baba said, 'Sagun, bring me soft cooked rice for breakfast tomorrow'. So the next morning I took some cooked rice, a *papad*, and some curd. Thus every day about 7 o' clock I took this for him. This was my daily routine for two years.

"One morning I found Baba standing near the *dhuni*. Baba turned to me and said, 'Have you put any *ghee* (clarified butter) on the rice?' I told him that I had not done so. Baba then said, 'Henceforth, put some *ghee* over the rice.' I did as I was bidden. Baba himself took a morsel or two from the plate and put it in the *dhuni*. Then he said, 'From now on bring *ghee* enriched rice, and put some of it in the *dhuni*, then give it to me."

Sagumeru states, "This became my daily routine. After Baba's *mahasamadhi*, I continued this *Vaishvadev puja* (offering boiled rice laden with *ghee* to *Agni dev* or *Dhuni Maa*.) I don't however bring breakfast now, but do offer *naivedya* in the Dwaraka Mai. At about noon I bring the *naivedya*, first put it in the *dhuni*, then I place some in front of Baba's photograph, after that put some in the *kolamba*, and the remaining I feed to stray dogs."

Baba through Sagunmeru taught us the proper way of making offerings. Sagunmeru used to give Baba breakfast and lunch. "मनावर तूप घातल्यावाचून, अन्नशुध्द केल्या वाचून म्हणजे वैश्व देव केल्यावाचून बाबाना (परमात्माला) न्याहारी किंवा नैवध देऊ नये।। "

(Baba's *updesh* or teaching was that the cooked rice should first be cleansed and purified by pouring some *ghee* on it. This is called *anna shudhi*. Then a little should be offered to *dhuni* or fire and this is *Vaishvadev puja*. After this it should be offered to God.)

This conversation took place between B V Dev and Sagunmeru. Dev in this article refers to a *shloka* (verse) from the *Dnayneshwari*. It's from Chapter 3, *Shloka* 24, *Ovi* 167 and 168. The translation is given below.

*Ovi* 167: "It is the tradition, that the ignorant should see how great masters like me behave in the world. If I fail in doing righteous duties, my followers would be ignorant. And their practical life will come into danger."

*Ovi* 168: "Therefore it's the responsibility of the great and knowledgeable masters to see that abandonment of duties do not occur, neither in their own life nor in the life of their followers."

Sagunmeru though not a high class Brahmin followed and dutifully carried on the *bodha paddhati* that Baba taught him.

Ref: *Sai Leela Margshrish Shake 1857. Ank 9. Year 12  (1936)*

*Leela 77:*  **A devotee named Prabhu takes a photograph of Baba**

Prabhu was a photographer, and he worked in a famous photo studio in Mumbai. On one occasion he visited Shirdi and wished to take a photograph of Baba. He had brought all the paraphernalia with him and decided to take the photograph without Baba's permission. So he did just that.

When he returned to Mumbai, he got the print developed. To his utter surprise, the photograph was that of his own guru, and not of Baba. From that experience he got a valuable lesson, that he should keep all his faith and devotion at his guru's feet.

Ref: *Shirdi che Sai Baba by Dr K B Gavankar*

*Leela 78:*  **Drop the wall, and that's enough**

On one occasion a group of devotees came to Shirdi. They had Baba's *darshan* and stayed for three days. They longed with all their hearts and souls to take a photograph of Baba, so they had brought their camera with them.

They knew that Baba usually did not allow his photograph to be taken. Therefore they requested Shama to seek Baba's permission, and Shama agreed to do so. Shama and the group waited near Sathe *wada*. Baba had gone to Lendi Baugh, and when he returned, Shama said, "*Deva*, these people want to take a photograph of you, so just stand there for a moment, while they do so."

Baba replied, "Tell these children not to take any photo. If they just tear down the wall that is between us then that is enough." When Baba says this he means a photograph would only depict his human form of 3 ½ cubit, whereas the devotees should look beyond that human form, i.e., his divinity or *nirgun roopa*, and lock it in their heart.

Ref: *Shirdi che Sai Baba by Dr K B Gavankar*

In *Shri Sai Satcharita* Chapter 35, the story of Kaka Mahajani and his friend is given. His friend comes to Shirdi on the condition that he will not bow at Baba's feet, nor give *dakshina*. Baba says, "Pull down the wall of the Teli, the wall of separateness between you and me." If the wall that defines you and me in worldly terms can be avoided then divinity will be perceived.

*Leela 79:*  # Baba asks Ghaisis for bhiksha of 53 rupees

One day R B Ghaisis had a vivid dream, where in Baba asked him for 53 rupees. He was a poor man and could not afford to give that amount at once. Diligently he saved 63 *annas*. This he did for 4 months, but somehow the money got spent on something or the other.

Then one day he met Dabolkar and told him about his dream and his inability to save that amount. Dabolkar explained the dream thus, "Baba does not want 53 coins from you. I think he is asking you to read the *Gurucharita* daily. This *pothi* has 53 chapters and that is the *dakshina*."

Ghaisis went and bought a *Shri Sai Satcharita* and started doing a *saptha*. That night he dreamt that thieves had made a hole in the wall of his home and entered it. Frightened out of his wits he screamed. His wife shook him and asked him what had happened. He told her about the dream.

It was a family tradition to read the *Gurucharita* daily, and do *saptha* of it often. That morning his son Sakharam told him that he had intended to do a *saptha* of the *Gurucharita* that week. They finally understood that Baba wanted them to continue with the tradition of their ancestors, i.e., to read the *Gurucharita* on a daily basis. And also to read *Shri Sai Satcharita*.          Ref: *Shirdi che Sai Baba by Dr K B Gavankar*

*Leela 80:* # Vakthirek Gyan

Baba saved the ironsmith's baby when she fell into the furnace at Nigoj. This *leela* is described in *Shri Sai Satcharita* Chapter 7. While saving the baby, Baba's hand was burnt badly. The only treatment for it was to tie it tightly. Early in the morning Bhagoji Schinde came to the Dwaraka Mai and did this.

Many of his devotees entreated him to take some medicines and get the hand examined by a doctor. But all these requests fell on deaf ears. Once when such a request was made, Baba said, "Get some good cow dung cakes, about a thousand or two thousand, then ignite them. When they are burning brightly put this body over it. (Baba pointed to his body while he said this) Then stand beside it to watch the fun. And see this body burn."

This is called *Vakthirek Gyan*. *Vakthi* means 'a human being or a person'. *Rek* means 'emptying or purging off', i.e., emptying yourself of *arishadvargas*. Possible meaning is that the 'I' is so caught up in this materialistic world, that the real 'I' is forgotten. Self-realised people can stand aside and watch their self burning, and witness an out of body experience.   Ref: *Shirdi che Sai Baba by Dr K B Gavankar*

*Leela 81:*   # Sagunmeru Naik

I t is appropriate to write a little about Sagun's life here as he was the living example of Baba's teachings.

Sagun was affluent; he had vast acres of land, farms, cattle and possessed his own home. His meeting with a fakir (Baba) was very interesting. He lived in Marma Goa, it was his daily routine to take the cattle to pasture, and then take them to the *vihir* (sort of a well) for a drink of water. While he was doing this chore he saw a fakir seated below a *peepul* tree. The fakir had on a *kafni* and a cloth tied around his head. When he looked at him, the fakir made a sign with his eyes. The sign was to beckon him to come near. Sagun could not understand it, and little did he realise that Baba had given him *drusti path*. *Drusti path* is transference of divine energy through the eyes. From that time he lost all his desire of living with his family.

## Sagun visits numerous pilgrim places

Sagun visited almost every place of pilgrimage in the south like Gangapur, Pandharpur and Narsobavadi. At Narsobavadi he stayed for about four months. There he met Shri Vasudevanand Sarasvati (Tembe Swami mentioned in *Shri Sai Satcharita* Chapter 51.) Tembe Swami said to him, "*Arre*, you are a child from the *Mota* (big) house." Here he refers to Baba as *mota*. Then Sagun went to south of Hyderabad, but because he looked like an unkempt *sanyasi*, the police harassed him. When they found that he was harmless, they actually gave him a place to stay, and made arrangements for his meals. Sagun finally reached Shirdi.

One day an affluent gentleman wanted to visit Shirdi, so Sagun accompanied him. When they went for *darshan*, Baba was returning from Lendi Baugh. There numerous devotees were waiting to have his *darshan*. Sagun also stood there, but a little away from the rest. Baba looked directly and in Kannada asked him three questions, "Why have you come? What are you going to do? Where are you going?" This had an immense impact on him, as no one knew its significance but him. There and then he decided never to leave Shirdi.

## Sagun does some business to take care of his expenses

'Hunger does not elude any one' this was very evident to him. So he did different businesses during his stay at Shirdi. I will not go into every detail of his business ventures but I will write Baba's *vaani* and blessings. He opened a tea and snack shop in front of the Dwaraka Mai. On the day of its opening he brought a *laddu* and some *chivda* on a plate and offered it to Baba. Baba took a pinch of each and said, "It's good. One must do some work and not sit idle. Do not worry I am there in your shop."

As the crowd started coming, he opened a *bhojanavali* (dining hall). He never forgot to offer *prasad bogh* to Baba. Sagunmeru was kind hearted, he saw to it that no one slept hungry in Shirdi. Whether the person was well off or not, a sadhu or a wayfarer, he gave that person a meal. Baba had once told him, '*भुकेल्या जीवाची भुक जाणावी. रिक्तहस्ते दारातून कुणाला पाठवू नये।।* "

"Feel the hunger of that person as if it's your own hunger. Do not send anyone empty-handed from your doorstep."

When Baba's *granth (Shri Sai Satcharita)* was published, he kept them in his shop and sold them. Lastly he got Girje, a photographer from Sholapur to give him photo prints of Baba. He got the prints framed and sold them.

## Some little known facts about this devotee

He came to Shirdi around 1908, and stayed in the same house for about 56 years. Never did he miss a single day of bringing *naivedya* for Baba. Even after Baba's *mahasamadhi*, he brought *naivedya* to the Dwaraka Mai daily, only the breakfast he omitted.

Baba called him *takki* (deceiver), but why Baba called this wonderful devotee by that name, only Baba knows. Even after Baba's *mahasamadhi* he continued doing *Vaishvadev puja*. Baba gave a lot of money to various devotees but did not give any money to Sagun. Never did he complain, or ask Baba why he did not give him any money. He did *niskam seva* (not expecting any reward).

Even when adversities befell him, he said, "Whether something is good or bad, it's Baba's wish." His life was a textbook picture of *nista* (faith) of Baba's *bodha paddhati*.

'फसलीही अभिलाषा नको।। जेवढे मिळेल त्यात समाधान मानून रहावे।। जेवढे शक्य असेल तेवढे दुस-याच्या उपयोगी पडावे।। उपयोगी पडतांना परतफेडीची इच्छा नसावी।। "

The meaning for the above is: 1. Do not have expectations and don't long for others to give you anything. 2. Be content with what you have. 3. Whatever is within your ability, do so to help others. 4. After helping others do not expect any returns or rewards. 5. When some one is hungry, feel as if you are starving, so give him food. 6. Do not send anyone empty-handed from your doorstep.

## Sagun is sick and at death's door, but recovers

Once Sagun was very ill, he was at death's door. This happened after Baba's *mahasamadhi*. The villagers were concerned and thought that there was no chance for his recovery. His faith in Baba did not waiver an iota. When he did recover and was able to walk about, he went straight to the Dwaraka Mai. And standing before Baba's portrait, with tears in his eyes said, "*Natha, Deva*, Baba, what a lot of trouble you take upon yourself for me. What difficulties you face for me!" This he cried out aloud, and every devotee who was there had tears in their eyes hearing it. Sagun took *samadhi* (expired) at the age of 85 in Shirdi. Unfortunately his *samadhi* is not made in Shirdi.

## Sagun finally realises when he met Baba

Once Sagun had an intense desire to visit his mother. He went to ask Baba for permission, when Baba said, 'तुझे आईबाप सर्व इथेच आहे, मी तुझी सर्व सोय इथे केली असतांना तुला काळजी कशाला।। "

"You father, mother and every one else are all here. *Arre*, when I went to your home, your mother gave me *shida* (uncooked grains and pulses)." Suddenly he realised that the fakir seated below the *peepul* tree in his village was Baba.

127

This in short is the life of a wonderful devotee, who finally became one with his Lord.     Ref: *Shri Sai Sagar Deepavali Visesh Ank. Year 2001*

*Leela 82:*     # Vaman Chintaman Mukhe

Vaman Chintaman Mukhe sent this letter to the *Sai Leela Magazine* on 11-07-1921 narrating his experiences. It is given below.

## Kaka Puranic is Mukhe's guru

Kaka Puranic was his *moksh* guru, i.e., Raghunath Maharaj of Dopeshwar. After Mukhe received *updesh* (initiation) from his guru, his mental outlook changed a lot. He took more interest in spirituality. To his amazement he started visiting various *sadgurus*. Then he desired to read the *Dnayneshwari*, which he did. In the *Dnayneshwari*, the love and devotion that Dnayneshwar had for his guru, Nivriti Nath, is described beautifully.

Mukhe also desired to have a guru whom he could love and respect like Dnayneshwar. Just at that time Kaka Puranic asked him to go to Shirdi, and meet Baba. Following his advice, he decided to go to Shirdi. At Shirdi his meeting with Baba was more than what he wished for. Baba lovingly made him sit near him, and blessed him. Just before going to the Dwaraka Mai he bought a *Sagunapasan* (*arati* book) and a photograph of Baba. He hoped with his heart and soul that Baba would sanctify these with his touch. Of course Baba knew this, so Baba asked him for both the *arati* book and photograph. Then Baba blessed them and handed them over to him. When Mukhe received them the vibrations were so strong that he was filled with ecstasy.

## Thieves enter his home in Pimpalgaon

Mukhe was a lawyer by profession. He resided in Pimpalgaon Baswanth, a small town in Niphad *talluqa*. There he practiced law.

128

Around 1916, plague broke out in Pimpalgaon, so he moved out of the *gaon*. He owned some farmlands on which he had built a small bungalow. So whenever there was an epidemic of plague, he and his family would stay there. In those days plague was rather rampant in those parts.

## Thieves steal his valuables

Once when it was well past midnight, four thieves attacked his home. They broke open the northern wall of his house. About a bricks length away from the opening that they had created hung Baba's photograph. Mukhe was fast asleep on a cot that was placed next to Baba's photograph. Through the opening one thief entered, while the others waited outside. The thief took a small trunk that was below his cot, and handed it over to his accomplices who were waiting outside. That trunk contained Rs 250/- in notes and some change. But more importantly it contained the promissory letter from his debtor for Rs 4,000/-.

There was another trunk in front of his cot that contained some gold trinkets, worth Rs 3,500/- and some silverware worth about Rs 500/-. While the thieves were moving that trunk, his sister-in-law who was sleeping nearby woke up, and started shouting, "Robbers have come." Through all this commotion Mukhe was fast asleep.

## Baba wakes Mukhe and informs him about the robbery

Although Mukhe was sound asleep, Baba was not. Baba came in his dream and said, "Wake up, they are taking your trunk." Hearing Baba's warning Mukhe jumped out of bed and he started shouting, "Beat these thieves." Finally the watchman also got up and joined in the shouting. Thus the robbers fled for their lives.

Mukhe then prostrated before Baba's photograph and thanked him for waking him up while the robbery was in progress. Later that day he sent one of his farm help to the police station to register the robbery. The police came to his home and inspected everything and the necessary paper work was done. Just after the police left, one of his farmers came, and informed him that his trunk was lying in the field. About a furlong away from his home, he retrieved the trunk.

Upon inspecting it, he found that the bundle of money was missing but the promissory note and property papers were intact.

## Bramachari Bua of Kopergaon comes to stay with Mukhe

A week after the theft, Bramachari Bua (a saint) visited his home and stayed with them for a few days. Mukhe was extremely happy as he loved saints. Mukhe took great care to make the saint's stay comfortable and pleasant. Bramachari Bua stayed for three days, and before leaving told Mukhe that he would recover his stolen articles.

The four thieves sold all the stolen goods to a *Marwadi*. Then they proceeded to rob another home and were caught. Simultaneously there was a raid on the *Marwadi's* house, and the stolen articles were found. After interrogation the *Marwadi* identified the thieves, who confessed everything. Thus Mukhe was called to identify and retrieve his articles. So it came to pass that he got back the bundle of notes and every stolen article.

## Mukhe has a vivid dream

A few days after the robbery Mukhe and his family decided to visit Shirdi. That night he had a vivid dream – he was in the Dwaraka Mai and doing Baba's *charan seva*. Baba was seated with Abdul Baba, and next to him there was a fakir. The fakir was of a fair complexion, and there was a brilliant aura surrounding him. Mukhe was intrigued, he had never seen that fakir before.

They took the evening train and reached Shirdi the next morning. He and his family went to the Dwaraka Mai, but Baba had gone in procession to Lendi Baugh. Mukhe and his family waited near the *Gurusthan* for his return. A short while later, Baba returned and Mukhe prostrated before him. Baba asked him to go to his lodging and to return later. Kaka Dixit who was there, invited Mukhe to be his guest. Mukhe accepted with gratitude.

About an hour later, he went to the Dwaraka Mai. To his utter surprise he found Abdul Baba seated with the fakir with brilliant countenance. He asked the other devotees there about the fakir. He learned that he was Abdul Baba's former guru.

Ref: *Sai Leela Jyeshth Shake 1845. Ank 4. Year 1 (1923)*

## *Leela 83:* **Baba goes to Ruigaon occasionally**

Baba rarely left Shirdi in the physical body. However, he did go to Rahatha, there he visited the home of Kushalchand Nagarseth. Their surname is Saand, though they were *Marwadis*, the *rinanubandh* between Baba and Kushalchand was deep. In *Shri Sai Satcharita* Chapter 8, the details are given. Baba gave them a small photograph of his which is still venerated by the family.

Often Baba went to Neemgaon, to visit Nana Sahib Dengle. The visit is described beautifully in *Shri Sai Satcharita* Chapter 5.

Occasionally Baba went to Ruigaon, which is on the opposite side of Neemgaon. Here there is an ancient *audumbar* tree. In front of it is a *Maruti* Mandir. The details of his visits there are unavailable, and one does not know what he did there.

### Baba taught in parables

Baba taught in parables, most of the time. Only the person for whom the *bodha paddhati* was meant understood it. Most of the other devotees thought that Baba was telling a story.

## *Leela 84:* **Parables**

### The grocer who had 3 pots of clarified butter

There was a grocer. He filled three pots with clarified butter (*ghee*). My *mahatara* (literally means 'old man', this term is also used to refer to the father) was with me, he said, "If the pots are placed before me. I will eat all the *ghee* at one sitting." At that very moment the grocer's brother called him to have his lunch. The grocer kept the pots inside the shop and locked the door. He said, "I'll give you roasted gram." I was with the *mahatara*. There were two other kids; they broke the rear wall of the shop. They gave the wall one kick and it fell down. Then they came in and ate the *ghee* from two of the pots. My *mahatara* made a sign to me, and I ate the *ghee* from the third pot. The grocer returned I told him about the *ghee*. The grocer found that there was no gold in the shop. They took all of us to the *Chavdi*, then the real robbers were caught, so they set me free. Then my `stomach hurt, I passed all the *ghee* in my stools. Then my *mahatara* cured me. The grocer kept me for two years.

Ref: *Sai Leela Aashad Shake 1845. Ank 5. Year 1 (1923)*

## The possible meaning

The grocer is *parabrahma*, who fills 3 pots with *ghee*. The 3 pots are the 3 karmas which are – (i) *Sanchita* (ii) *Agami* (iii) *Prarabdha*. The meaning of *Sanchita* is what any *vastu* has earned during the innumerable past lives. The word *vastu* is used here to mean a person that has a higher level of thinking. Or one who knows and realises that the parabrahma is in everything. In *Shri Sai Satcharita* Chapter 3, *Ovi* 85, Baba says, "Whatever exists in the sentient and insentient Universe that has a name, a form, or a shape is only me, bedecked in the eightfold *Prakriti*. It is also my own creation." *Agami* means what any *vastu* earns due to present actions and *Prarabdha* means the fruits of his karmas are yielding results in the present life.

*Mahatara* is the *sadguru*, for only he can eat all the 3 pots of *ghee* (karmas) at one sitting. For he is a self-realised soul, no karma will attach itself onto him as he is beyond all this. In Sanskrit, *bhuj* is the *dhatu* for *bhakti*; *bhuj* means to eat. The *parabrahma's* food is the sincere, affectionate devotion which is full of love.

Any *vastu* being *parabrahma* himself, all *vastus* are siblings of *parabrahma*. So the brother calling the grocer to have lunch means a devoted *vastu* offering his devotion. Keeping the pots inside and locking the door means placing of karmas in any *vastu*. Roasted gram produces gas so it removes intoxicated, poisonous and bad contents from the body. Giving roasted gram means bestowing knowledge that will remove *maya*. This is possible as the *vastu* is with the old man 'the *sadguru*'.

The other 2 kids are *viveka* and *vairagya*. Only *viveka* and *vairagya* can kick the wall of *ajnana* (ignorance) and make it fall. Naturally everything becomes open, i.e., *akash tatva*. All *vastus* are made up of *panchabhootas – prithvi, aapas* (jal), *vayu, agni* and *akash*. All the other 4 can be felt except *akash*. That means nothing or *shoonya* which in reality is life. Now the *vastu's karma, sanchita* and *agami* are eaten by *viveka* and *vairagya*. Then the *sadguru* makes a sign, i.e., *kripa* and *shiksha*, so this *vastu* can eat the other pot of *ghee*, i.e., *prarabdha* also.

Then he tells about the *ghee* which means direct communication with the *parabrahma*. 'No gold in the shop' means there is no urge for materialistic and worldly desires. 'They go to the *Chavdi*' means introspection, the process of knowing the self. The robbers are the *arishadvargas*. When they are caught the real self is free. It is always free even when it's under chains.

'Hurting of the stomach' is relieving the self from *bandhans* through *sadhana* so that *prarabdha* is purged out. 'The old man cured me', i.e., bestowing of *kripa dristi* which has a cooling effect like that of moonlight. 'Keeping him for two years' means Baba as Ram in *tetrayug* and Krishna in *dwaparayug*.

This is the possible meaning, but many of you may find other meanings. *Ref: Sai Leela Aashad Shake 1845. Ank 5. Year 1 (1923)*

## The boy cries time and again

There was a farmer's son, he came to the *wada*. There he grew up. He stayed for 12 years, and then he started crying. He wanted to go to his parents so he cried. The *Badshah* (Emperor) told him that there were many *wadas* so he could stay in any of them. Then the *Badshah* gave him a *wada*. After a while the boy started crying again. The *Badshah* gave him his daughter, they got married. The wife did not get any children, so the *Badshah* reasoned with him and pacified him. Still he left. The *Badshah* gave him gold sovereigns because he was a rich man. The farmer's son's name was Rehila. He then, married a girl from his caste. Then again he started crying.

The *Badshah* was willing to give his life for him. He gave him his *wada*, his daughter, still he wanted to go to his parents. The need for *samsaric* life did not leave him. The *Badshah* was a great man, he gave him a lot of gold. If he had listened to the *Badshah*, he would have gotten his kingdom.   Ref: *Sai Leela Aashad Shake 1845. Ank 5. Year 1 (1923)*

## The possible meaning

When a person leaves his or her mortal body, the *jeev atma* is in this world for 12 days. This is a strong belief.

The child who is crying is the a*tma*. The 12 years is the twelve days that the a*tma* wanders about in this world. The a*tma* cries as it wants to meet and unite with the *parabrahma*. But the *Badshah* (*parabrahma*) lures him and entices him by giving the huge *wada*. The beautiful *wada* is a beautiful body to live in.

The *Badshah* then gives him wealth in the form of materialistic wealth yet the *atma* cries. So he gives his daughter in marriage. That is *maya*, his own creation and makes the *atma* in this body be totally submerged in worldly life or *samsaric jeevan*, which is by way of marriage.

Again the *atma* cries. His daughter does not bear any children could mean unaffected by the materialistic world. So he marries another lady and that is self-realisation.

Ref: *Sai Leela Aashad Shake 1845. Ank 5. Year 1 (1923)*

## The parable of the 4 brothers

There were 4 brothers. Two of the brothers went to a village. They were farmers, there they met a wise mature lady. The girl was Kabir's. They bought some farming machinery and implements from her. They made a sign to her and she left.   They took her with them. They then proceeded to their village. I was small so too went with them. In their village the villagers went on a fact finding mission. And instilled fear in them.   Then two of them took the lady, and went on top of a hill. I followed them. The lady had two children. She searched and then found out where her parents were. Some of the people said take the lady and kill the brothers. Her parents said, "They have two kids. Let them be."

Ref: *Sai Leela Chaitra Shake 1845. Ank 1. Year 1 (1923)*

## The possible meaning

The 4 brothers represent *manas* (mind), *budhi* (intelligence), *aham* (ego) and *chitta* (conscious mind) Two brothers are *manas* and *budhi*, who go to their village; they make an inward journey. Every being is a farmer who does *sadhana* to find the eternal question, 'Who am I'. The two brothers find the wise mature lady, she is *jnana* (knowledge). She was Kabir's, indeed Kabir is a self-realised soul or *parabrahma*. She belonged to him. They bought farming machinery and implements from *jnana*. That means getting (buying) *sadguru krupa* in the *sadhana marg*.

Once the *sadhana marg* is blessed by *sadguru krupa*, it leads to knowledge of *nitya* (knowledge of the transient) and *Anyta Vivek* (intransient nature of the materialistic world). They went to their village or discipline. They took discipline, together with *manas, budhi, jnana*, and started leading a day-to-day life.

*Aham* (I went with them) also travels with them (*manas* and *budhi*) to know the real 'I'. The fact finding mission is *chitta* and *arshidvargas*, who lure *manas, budhi* and *aham* to see if they are really disciplined.

The disciplined journey of *manas, budhi* and *aham* leads to the non-existence of the false 'I'. The loss of the false identity injects fear in the mind, as false 'I' needs to be assured of its identity.

By *Yoga marga* the *Shakskar Kundalani* is awoken. She came to know where her parents were, i.e., *jnana* realises *Shakshar Kundalani*. The parents' place, the seat of realisation, is *Shakshar Kundalani*.

They beget two children. First is *nirukti* which is to be unaffected by this materialistic world. The second is Self-realisation.

Ref: *Sai Leela Aashad Shake 1845. Ank 5. Year 1 (1923)*

I hope I have deciphered some of this parable, while you may find some other meanings.

## Dakshina

The word *dakshina* means 'sacrificial fees'.

### Types of dakshinas

There are 2 types of *dakshinas*. 1. *Vwharik* is a business transaction. 2. *Aavwharik* is *adhyatmic* or spiritual.

The *shastras* teach us that we should not go to meet god, guru or a king empty-handed. So we usually bring a coconut, bananas, or some fruits, flowers, sugar candy and *pedas*, as an offering. Importantly when we offer money, this is considered as business transaction type of *dakshina*.

When we take *deksha* from a guru, he blows a mantra in our ear. Then we do his *pad puja* and give him *dakshina*, this is considered as an *adhyatmic dakshina*.

Initially Baba did not ask any one for *dakshina*. He lived the life of a fakir. The Dwaraka Mai was an old dilapidated mosque. His belongings were few, all he possessed was a sack for his seat, a cloth to cover his head, a *kafni*, a *langoti*, a *khapar* (bowl used for dry food), a tin tumrel (for liquids) and his *satka*. This was his *samsar*. Hence he had no need for collecting money.

He begged for food from certain houses, and ate whatever was given to him as *bhiksha*. For his *chillum* he got tobacco from the village. So also did he get wood for his *dhuni*, and oil for his lamps from a few shopkeepers. Hence there was no need for money. The villagers did not pay any heed to him, they thought he was a mad fakir.

## Baba started asking for dakshina

When devotees from Mumbai and other places started visiting Shirdi, and his divinity was quite evident, the villagers came for his *darshan*. His fame spread far and wide. People heard that an *Awalia* had manifested in Shirdi, they came in droves. It was then that Baba started asking for *dakshina*.

His method of asking for *dakshina* was unique. He did not ask every one for *dakshina*. If a devotee offered *dakshina*, sometimes he accepted it and at other times he did not accept it. Many a devotee wished that Baba would ask him and he would give the *dakshina*. But Baba may or may not have asked him for *dakshina*.

If the person was disinclined to give *dakshina* Baba did not ask him for it. If he offered it Baba did not accept it. If he placed it there (traditionally *dakshina* is placed at the feet of the saint) Baba would ask him to take it away without touching it. He did not take *dakshina* from solely the wealthy people. He asked it from everyone, even females and children, e.g. Mrs Tarkhad. Baba asked her to give him Rs 6, i.e., the 6 internal enemies (*Shri Sai Satcharita* Chapter 9). From children as well, e.g. he asked Gavankar for 2 paisa (*shradha* and *saburi*), this transaction was completed by Gavankar saying it's 'given' and Baba saying it's 'accepted'.

## What did Baba do with the dakshina

Many a time Baba gave back a portion of the *dakshina* to the devotee and said, "This is my money that I give you. Now keep it in a safe place. If you choose to keep it in the *devera*, then perform daily *puja* to it." Some times when a devotee gave a certain amount, Baba demanded the same amount again. He even fought with the devotee and got double the original amount. When Dr Gavankar's guru went for *darshan* he gave Baba 2 rupees as *dakshina*. Baba demanded and fought till he got 4 rupees, i.e., double the amount.

Every day he collected about 200-300 rupees, this he kept in his pocket. Of the *dakshina* he did not spend a single *anna* on himself. He gave 10 to 100 rupees to certain devotees. From the remaining amount he bought baskets of mangoes, guavas, bananas and sugarcanes, and distributed it. *Kirtankars*, *bhikshuks*, jugglers and magicians all benefited from it. He gave large amounts to them depending on their skill. In the evening he did not own a single pie.

When Baba took *dakshina* there was a lesson in it. He tested the person giving it. Was he giving it willingly? Was his *atma* saddened by the thought of having to part with his money? Was his attachment to money deep? Was there a chance that it would lessen over time? He taught these things by demanding *dakshina*. The amount he took, he returned it a hundredfold. Just as Krishna asked Draupati for food when she had little to eat let alone give food to anybody. Then she gave a grain of rice, later she became so affluent, that she could feed a multitude of sadhus.

## Guru Dakshina

The second type of *dakshina* is guru *dakshina* where the guru gives mantra *updesh* and the disciple gives *dakshina*. But the *dakshina* need not necessarily be money. Baba often asked for *dakshina* from the *pothi* the devotee was reading.

## The dakshina of nista and saburi

In Chapters 18 and 19 of *Shri Sai Satcharita* the story of Sathe, Radhabai Deshmuk and Dabolkar is given and guru's grace is explained. This is an apt example of guru *dakshina*.

Around 1917, a householder named Sathe came to Shirdi. The reason for his visit was a troubled mind because of huge losses in his business. The very moment he saw Baba, his mind lost its restlessness, and he became calm and serene. He prostrated at Baba's feet and kissed them.

Of his own accord he started a *saptha* of the *Gurucharita*. With love, devotion and a calm mind he completed the reading in 7 days. That night he had a dream, he saw himself seated on the top floor of his building reading the *Gurucharita*. Then Baba came with a *Gurucharita* in his hand and sat beside him. Then Baba explained the portion he was reading, like a mother would to a child. He was filled with peace and joy. The next day he related his dream, to Dixit. Sathe requested him to ask Baba whether he should do another *saptha*.

Baba said, "He should do another *saptha*. By reading the *Gurucharita*, the mind becomes pure, peaceful and his spiritual welfare is secure. The Lord will be pleased and break the shackles that bind one to the materialistic world."

Dabolkar was seated at Baba's feet, and he thought, 'Sathe is blessed by merely reading the *Gurucharita* for 7 days, while I have been reading it for 40 years without being blessed. His reading bears fruit while mine does not.' As soon as this thought crossed his mind Baba asked him to go to Shama's house. Baba asked Dabolkar to bring *dakshina* from him and sit a while and chat with him.

Shama told him the story of Radhabai Deshmuk. Radhabai was an old lady who came to Shirdi with some devotee's from Sangamnere. The moment she saw Baba's luminous form she made up her mind to obtain guru mantra from him. In her determination to do so, she fasted without ingesting any sort of food or water. Thus three days passed. Shama was concerned about her health. He told Baba this, "That old lady is determined to get a guru mantra from you and till that time she would starve. Even if she dies, it does not matter to her. In the event if she dies, every one will blame you. Because you did not give her the mantra *updesh*. Call her and tell her some thing."

## The story of Radhabai Deshmuk

Heeding Shama's advice Baba spoke to her. "Mother, I had a guru who was loving and divine. I had no dearth of food, clothing and shelter. He provided me with everything. He did not care for any worldly possessions. He was a very spiritual guru.

"I stayed with him for 12 years, serving him from morning to night. I loved him with my heart and soul, and I thought of nothing else. My guru was the only thought, and the only *sadhana*, I had. He got my head shaved and asked me to give 2 paisa as *dakshina*. Mother, these 2 paise were not monetary coins. What he asked for was *nista* and *saburi* (the meaning of *nista* is loyalty, faith, reliance and integrity. *Saburi* is fortitude and courageous patience.) These 2 paise I gave willingly. My guru did not have any expectations, from me. He guarded me and protected me from harm. When he did not whisper any mantra in my ear, how can I give you any mantra.

"There are no words by which I can describe the greatness of my guru. I willingly and happily gave him these 2 paise. He was not greedy and did not expect me to give him any thing other than *nista* and *saburi*. Whether I was at his feet or in a far off place I did not feel the lack of his love and grace. My guru was like the mother tortoise, who though on opposite bank, nurtures and gives sustenance to her young ones, just by glancing lovingly at them.

"Mother, keep this story locked in your heart, and don't bother with incantations and mantras. Day and night my only thought was that off my guru. So think day and night solely of your guru. Mother keep your attention focussed on me and me alone, and your spiritual goal will be achieved."

Just as Shama finished telling Dabolkar this wonderful story the bell of the Dwaraka Mai rang so they went to attend the *arati*. Baba was eager to hear what they had spoken about. Dabolkar narrated the story to Baba. Just as he finished doing so the *arati* ended, and Jog gave Baba sugar candy as *prasad*. Baba in turn handed it to

Dabolkar and said, "Forever keep this story in your heart and soul, and your mental state will be as sweet as this candy. Your spiritual goal will be achieved. And you will blessed a million times."

In this *leela*, guru *dakshina* is given by Sathe in the form of *parayan* of the *Gurucharita*. Baba blesses him with the dream vision, where in Baba explains the chapter to him. Shama gives 15 namaskars in lieu of the 15 rupees. Baba blesses him by making him his spokesman. Dabolkar gives guru *dakshina* of *nista* and *saburi* from this story. Baba blesses him sugar candy and showing him the way to total guru *bhakti*.

## Kashiram Shimpi gives Baba 2 paisa daily

Any devotee giving *dakshina* should not be proud that he is giving the *dakshina*, and he can afford to do so. Nor should the devotee feel the guru depends on the *dakshina* given. An apt example of this is Kashiram Shimpi. He came into Baba's contact from the very beginning. At that time Baba did not ask for *dakshina* nor did any one give it to him. However, Kashiram gave Baba 2 paise every day. If for any reason Baba did not accept it he felt disappointed and sad. Often his eyes welled with tears when Baba refused to accept it.

The omniscient Baba, however knew that Kashiram's pride was hurt. Baba then asked him for *dakshina* at all times, till he ran out of money. One day Kashiram told Baba that he did not have the money. Baba asked him to borrow it from the grocer. After a few days the grocer refused to lend him the money. It was only then that he realised the lesson in it. Baba did not depend on his *dakshina* for his meagre needs. He also realised that pride had slowly but surely taken over his whole being. Most importantly that Baba was not an ordinary human being like himself, but that Baba was *parabrahma,* he was the donor and the receiver, and every action was through him. From that moment his fortune returned and he became wealthy, but humble.

On one occasion Kashiram was returning from Newsari. He had gone to sell some bales of cloth. After the transaction was successfully completed, he was returning home with a lot of cash. Kashiram was riding on a horse, and he was attacked by a group of dacoits.

140

Though he was all alone he fought with all his might, he was unable to ward off their fierce attack. The leader of the band struck him on his head with an axe. Kashiram fell down unconscious. The leader thought that he was dead and they left.

At Shirdi, Baba let out a stream of abuses, and shook his *satka* at some unseen object. In fact he was battling with the band on Kashiram's behalf. Thus the *sadguru* saved his life, and Kashiram slowly recovered from his injuries.

## Baba takes on the fever of Gajanan Naverkar

The Guru when he takes *dakshina* looks after both the spiritual, materialistic and well being of the devotee, i.e., he looks after his welfare in totality.

Once a devotee named Gajanan Naverkar was suffering from high and continuous fever. He sent his son to Shirdi with *dakshina* of 500 rupees. His son went to the Dwaraka Mai, and gave Baba the 500 rupees. The moment the money touched Baba's hand Baba got high fever and started shivering.

A devotee seated next to Baba saw him shivering and asked him how he got the high fever all of a sudden. Baba replied, "When I accept *dakshina* from any one, I have to carry all his burdens, whether spiritual, materialistic or physical (health)."

## Mrs Purandhare

On one of his visits to Shirdi, Purandhare was doing Baba's *charan seva*, while his wife was seated in front of Baba. Looking directly at her Baba said, "Go quickly and give me all the money you have. I don't have any money with me." At once Mrs Purandhare got up, and took the keys from her husband and went to their lodge.

The couple had saved money in a box for Lakshmi *puja*. She emptied the box and laid the entire sum at Baba's feet. "Today you have looted your own home and given the entire sum to me. But did it ever cross your mind that your husband would be angry with you?" said Baba. Mrs Purandhare replied, "He will never be angry with me. Besides I am giving the money to you, that will make him extremely happy. If I gave the money to some one else also, he will not be offended."

141

Then Baba said, "Your *Dev* (husband) is a good person. Do not ever hurt or offend him, as he is mine." Innocently Mrs Purandhare asked, "Baba, who do I belong to?"

"*Arre*, you are also mine. You will lack nothing in your life. Don't be afraid, and let you mind remain just as it is. Allah will be pleased, as he is the saviour of the poor. Take good care of your family and your children. Now take this *udi* and go."

## Leela 85: Baba asks Butti to get 16½ rupees as dakshina from Dixit

One day Dixit and Bhate were reading the *Eknath Bhagwat*. It was a daily ritual for Dixit to read the *pothi* as Baba had advised him to do so. Bapu Sahib joined them, and said, "I have come from the Dwaraka Mai with the message that Baba has asked me to bring Rs 16½ from you. He also insisted that I bring back only 16½ rupees, and nothing less. He then said I should sit with you and listen to the portion being read. Again and again he emphasised that I bring Rs 16½ and not 16 rupees."

At that time Dixit, had only 1 rupee and that too was given by Baba on *Gurupurnima*. So he said, "Bapu Sahib take my humble prostrations in lieu of the 16½ rupees. We are about to start reading the daily portion of the *Bhagwat*. You are welcome to join us." So Bapu Sahib sat with them and heard what they were reading. "कायेन वाचा मनसेंद्रियैर्वा, बुध्यात्मना वा प्रकृती स्वभावन करोमि यद्यत्सकल परस्मै, नारायणायेति समर्वयामि ।।३।।"

"*Kayena vacha manasendriyairva, buddhayatmana va prakrti svabhavat. Karomi yadyat sakalam parasmai. Narayana yeti samarpayami.*"

It is apt to give some insights into this *shloka* here. The Nav Naths of the Rishab family, Kavi is one of them, expounded the principals of the *Bhagwat Dhram* to King Janak. The king asks them how to cross the ocean of life. Kavi explains what the *Bhagwat Dhram* is. The substance of the exposition is that in this *Kali Yug* the only means of liberation is remembrance of Hari's name and surrendering in totality to the Guru's feet.

This verse says, 'The entire *kayena* means skin or touch, the tongue or speech (*vacha*). The *manas* or mind and thought. The *indryias* or senses, the *budhi* or intellect, the *atma* or soul, the constitution or temperament. All the actions done by them should be surrendered to Lord Narayan. This amounts to complete or total surrender.'

Eknath Maharaj has written a knowledgeable thesis on this verse. Dixit had read and reread this so he told Bapu Sahib about it, just as he had finished doing so some one came to call Bapu Sahib to go to Dwaraka Mai. Intuitively Dixit knew that this verse was connected with the meaning of 16½ rupees.

He gave them numbers or marks and added them up. They are as follows: Skin or touch (1) Tongue or speech (1) Mind or thought (1) *Indryias* or the senses (10) *Budhi* or intellect (1) *Ahamkar* or ego (1) *Prakrati* or temperament ½ = 15½

But Baba repeatedly said, "Bring 16½ and not 16." It was impossible for Baba to be wrong so Dixit started thinking about it seriously. The meaning of it was that the nature and temperament of the individual is rather responsible for deeds done by that person.

Most of the karma or acts done in life are 'action orientated', i.e., a person may do a good deed with the intention of helping some one. These deeds are offered to god. Indeed they are already accepted by god. But those deeds that happen instinctively and by way of one's nature, they are harder to offer to god. Indeed it's god himself, who enables these deeds to occur.

If only every deed or action could be performed without a goal or motive, and the fruit of it not be sought (*nishkam* karma), the person is well on his way to spirituality. The person feels that such acts are ordained by god and he is but the instrument for its fruition, then the person is spiritual. Further if the person knows that god is the Master who ordains, that these actions be done, and I am but the instrument, he is very spiritual.

Nath Maharaj elaborates this further by giving an example. Once a *munim* conducted a business deal of one crore rupees. He knew that the money was not his but belonged to his Master. The *munim* was the instrument for this deal, and he carried it out according to the wish of his Master. The success of the deal, along with the money, belonged to his Master. The Master in this parable was God, and the *munim* the individual person. The success of the deal belonged to the Master, there was no pride involved as the huge sum of money did not belong to the *munim*.

Since god is the doer, there is no need to offer it back to him. Such a person is truly spiritual.

*Leela 86:* # Dinkar Mahadev Sapatnekar

Dinkar was born on the 14th of July 1918, fortunate was he to be born before Baba took *mahasamadhi*. His parents Mahadev and Parvatibai resided in Akkalkot, where Dinkar was born. In *Shri Sai Satcharita* Chapter 48, the story of his father's visit to Shirdi is given. On that visit Baba rebuked and told him to 'Get out'.

A year later they visited Shirdi again and Baba blessed them, and eight children were born to them. The oldest was Murlidhar, then Bhaskar (they are mentioned in the *Shri Sai Satcharita* Chapter 48, *Ovi* 152) and after him Dinkar. His mother took each one of them when they were but two months old and placed them at Baba's feet.

Dinkar narrated an interesting story about his first visit to Shirdi. His mother placed him at Baba's feet. Baba picked up the child and tossed him up in the air and caught him. Then Baba handed him to his mother. The rest of the devotees were surprised to see that nothing untoward had happened to the child who was blissfully happy.

## Dinkar's education and profession

Dinkar was highly educated; he studied both in Marathi and English medium. He did his matriculation in English. From Ferguson College, Poona he did M.A. and LL.B. He was commissioned by the Army during the war. He was very successful professionally and worked as a pleader, advocate, government public prosecutor and judge. He finally retired in 1981 as a Professor of law from Symbiosis College, Pune.

Vimla Kuluker of Pandharpur married him in 1942. They had 4 children who are well qualified and professionally successful.

After 1913 the Sapatnekar's often visited Shirdi, and Baba's grace was on them. Whenever there was childbirth, Sapatnekar would hold Baba's photograph on his shoulder, and pray. As soon as tears rolled down his cheeks the delivery would take place effortlessly.

He states that time and again Baba pulled him out of the jaws of death like when he was in the Army or while hunting. Dinkar was an excellent hunter, but he did not hunt for pleasure. The villagers would request him to kill a tiger as it devoured their cattle, or caused harm, only then would he kill that tiger.

Dinkar lives in Shivaji Nager, Pune. Although he had an attack of Hemiplegia and fractured his femur, his eyes and tone of voice tells of his intense and enduring faith in Baba.

Ref: *The above material was related by Dinkar himself*

# Dr Keshev Bhagvan Gavankar

His ancestors hailed from Aarnala, a small town near Wasai. His ancestors were *Ganpathi upasaks* and were abundantly blessed by *Ganpathi*. In fact the whole family was very spiritual.

His father, Bhagvan, worked as a contractor, selling coal and wood for fuel. Thus he was hardly at home, as he went to the forest to procure fossils. They lived in a large joint family, and looked after each other.

## Gavankar's birth and christening ceremony

He was born in *Vaishak shukla paksh, Shake* 1828, Saturday the 28th of April. His uncle Vitthal Kaka, knew a good astrologer, called Vithoba Anna Purandhare, who made his horoscope. He was pleasantly surprised to see it and told the family that the child was destined to be a great saint.

A suitable *muhurat* was found for the christening ceremony, and all their friends and relatives gathered together. The father decided to name him Ram, while others suggested the name Madhukar. It was agreed that the name would be Ram. Some time prior to placing the child in the cradle for the christening, the child started crying uncontrollably. The doctor checked him but found nothing wrong with him. Then his uncle looked at the horoscope again and found that the name ought to start with 'Ke'. His uncle then whispered in his ear, "We will name you Keshev, O.K.", and the baby stopped crying.

## The cradle catches on fire but Keshev is unharmed

One night Keshev was sleeping in the cradle, it was past midnight. His mother wanted to check on him, but she was not fully awake. It was pitch dark, so she decided to light the lantern. While doing so, she accidently dropped the lighted match on Keshev's bed clothes and it caught fire. With difficulty the fire was put out, but the child was unscathed and safe.

## Keshev's childhood

Keshev's childhood was a happy one. He was the favourite of his uncle Vitthalpanth and aunt Tammabai. His parents dotted on him, and he was the apple of their eyes. Keshev played and frolicked like the other children in his neighbourhood.

His initiation into education was with the mantra *'Shri Ganeshyaa namaha. Aum nama sidha'*. When Keshev was 7 years old he started going to school.

## Keshev gets 'empyema' and is very sick

One day Keshev returned from school with fever and cough. His mother made him comfortable, and laid him in his bed. She checked him a little while later and by that time he was 'burning with high fever'. The doctor was summoned, and the diagnosis was 'empyema'. His chest was congested and full of puss.

The illness was fulminant, and daily Keshev ran a temperature of 104 degrees. Many remedies were given to him, but there was no sign of improvement. Various doctors came and examined him. Ultimately the summoned Dr Badkamkar M.D. and Dr Rao suggested surgery. Vitthal Kaka, his uncle, took more opinions. All but two of the doctors suggested surgery.

When Dr Badkamkar asked for his consent for surgery, Vitthal Kaka did not consent. He said that the surgery would cause Keshev a great deal of pain and suffering. Besides there was no surety that he would recover. Thus three months went by, and the family lost hope of his ever recovering.

## Baba saves Keshev

Yashvantrao Dabolkar, happened to visit Shirdi along with his father-in-law Anna Sahib Dabolkar. He returned to Mumbai with Baba's *udi, padtirth* and Baba's photograph. Immediately he went to Keshev's home and gave Vitthal Kaka all the precious things he had brought with him. Then he said, "Kaka, for a long time various remedies have been tried on Keshev, but of no avail. Why don't you resort to Baba, take a vow of some sort, and fulfil it when he recovers."

## Vitthal Kaka liked the suggestion

With great reverence Vitthal Kaka placed Baba's photograph on the table. He lit a lamp, burnt *dhup*, did *arati*, and garlanded the photograph. Lastly, he placed his head at Baba's feet and said, "Hey, *Deva di dev*, I have never met you. I have only heard of your kindness and compassion. My grandson, Keshev, is at death's door, I beseech you to cure him with this prayer, I also offer this coconut. If he recovers I vow to offer you 5 *seers* of *peda*." Then he took the *udi* and *tirth*, touched these to Baba's feet and went to Keshev. At that time Keshev was unconscious, so he put a drop of *tirth* in his mouth, applied *udi* on his forehead and placed the photograph on his chest.

## Tammabai dreams of Baba

It was usual for Vitthal Kaka and Tammabai to sit at Keshev's bedside. It was past midnight at that time, and Tammabai dozed off. Then she had a vivid dream, in that dream Baba came to her home and asked her for a coconut. Then he went to Keshev's bedside, and passed his hand over his body. Baba then turned around, and said, "Allah *bhalla karega*." There ended the dream, and Baba left.

Tammabai got up and checked Keshev, he seemed cold. Startled, she started crying loudly, for she thought that Keshev had died. This woke the rest of the family and they came running to see what had happened. Dr Galvankar, who was sleeping upstairs, also came down. He examined Keshev, his pulse was regular and his fever had come down, thus he had cooled off. He reassured the family and every one went back to sleep.

The next morning Dr Galvankar found that Keshev's vest was wet and stuck to his chest. He cut the vest and found a small hole below his right nipple, and from it puss was oozing out. He applied pressure around it, and a lot of blood mixed with puss came out. After this was drained, Keshev recovered slowly but surely. Soon he resumed going back to school.

Ref: *Prabhav Shri Sai cha, Dr K B Gavankar yanche jeevan charita*

## Keshev finally meets Baba

Gradually, Keshev regained his health. Like any other child he went to school, and played with other children.

It is quite common for people to take a vow, when they are in trouble. But fulfilling it immediately is not always possible, either they forget it, or due to some circumstances are unable to fulfil it at once. This is exactly what happened with Vitthal Kaka.

After 5 years, in the month of January of 1918, they finally made the pilgrimage to Shirdi. Keshev accompanied his youngest uncle, Ramchandrapanth and aunt Tammabai.

They went to the Dwaraka Mai, many devotees were standing before Baba, so he and his family also stood beside them. Baba turned and looked at Keshev and beckoned him to come close. Then Baba said, "*Arre*, where are my *pedas*?" Ramchandrapanth went forward and gave the packet of *pedas* to Keshev.

Though the *pedas* were exactly 5 *seers* as per the vow, a few more *pedas* were added. Baba took the packet from Keshev's hand. He then gave 4 *pedas* to Keshev, and devoured the whole lot at one sitting. Shama who was nearby said, "*Deva*, what is this? You have eaten all the *pedas* yourself." Baba replied, "This child has starved me for 5 years."

Five years ago Keshev was at death's door, and Baba in a dream vision had cured Keshev.

Ref: *Prabhav Shri Sai cha, Anna Sahib Gavankar yanche jeevan charita*

## Baba blesses Keshev

Just prior to his visit to Shirdi, Keshev had his thread ceremony. His head was shaved except for the tuft (Shendy) of hair. Suddenly Baba caught Keshev's *shendy*, and with a great deal of force, pulled his head, and placed it on his feet.

Keshev saw a brilliant light, and quivers went down his spine. He was shaking and shivering at the same time. Thus Baba blessed this child.

## Baba asks Keshev for dakshina of 2 paise

Baba looked into Keshev's eyes and asked him for *dakshina* of 2 paise. Shama who was next to Keshev took his hand and extended it towards Baba. The gesture was as if Keshev was giving Baba the *dakshina*. Baba also extended his right hand, then Shama told Keshev to say *'Diyia'*, (I have given it).

Baba made a gesture of receiving it and said, "*Liyia*" (I have received it). Then he made a gesture of putting it safely in the pocket of his *kafni*. Then swiftly he took off his *kafni* and covered Keshev with it. All this time Keshev was in ecstacy, and his body was still quivering.

Every one felt Keshev was too young to receive Baba's *maha prasad*, the *kafni*. Shama intervened on Keshev's behalf and said, "*Deva*, let me keep this *kafni* for Keshev. When he is older I will give it to him." This is what Shama did, he gave it to Keshev at a later date. His descendants have the *kafni* and it's well preserved.

Ref: *Prabhav Shri Sai cha, Anna Sahib Gavankar yanche jeevan charita*

## Events at Shirdi that transformed Gavankar's life

On the very first day of his visit to Shirdi, Keshev went for Baba's *darshan*. Baba took a banana, peeled it and fed him just as one would feed a small child.

On the fifth day Keshev went for *darshan* early in the morning. Baba was sitting in front of the *dhuni*, and Bhagoji was untying his bandages. As soon as Baba noticed Keshev standing there, Baba called him to come near, and sit in front of him. Then swiftly, and with a great deal of force Baba slapped Keshev across his face. So forceful was the slap that Keshev's cap flew off.

On the 7th day, he and his family went to seek permission to leave. The rest of his family stood and did namaskar. Keshev also did the same; Baba held his hand and pulled him to a sitting position. Then Baba gave him a stinging slap across his face. Baba then gave him a palm full of *udi* and said, "Go my son; Allah will be good to you." With this blessing Keshev and his family returned home.

Ref: *Prabhav Sai cha, Anna Sahib Gavankar's jeevan charita*

150

## Baba gives Dr Gavankar a Ram murti

In the year 1938, Dr Gavankar got a vivid dream, in it Baba appeared and said, "Baala (child) what can I do for you? Henceforth start celebrating *Ram navami utsav*. And tie my cradle." So the first *Ram navami utsav* was started in *Chaitra shud padva* by the Hindu calendar.

The doctor got a beautiful cradle made; now all that remained was to get an equally beautiful *murti*. All his friends and relatives searched high and low for the *murti*, for nearly two months. Alas! it could not be found, finally it was decided to place a photograph of Shri Ram in the cradle. This was done and the function started, but Gavankar was dissatisfied.

He went and sat in front of Baba's photograph and cried, "*Deva*, according to your wishes I have started the *Ram navami utsav*, but I cannot find a *murti* of Ram to place in the cradle, and until I find one I will stop eating any food." Water was all that he ingested, but his daily routine was the same as before.

That year *Ram navami* was on Saturday, and it was Thursday and still no *murti* was found. As usual he went to his clinic, it was full of patients. They were seated according to their turn, amongst them was a new patient that he had not seen before. The doctor went to him and inquired about his health. He replied, "I will wait for my turn and then meet you."

When his turn came he stood in front of the doctor. He had on a shirt and coat on top of a *dhotar* with a *punari pagdi* on his head, and wore *punari* shoes. The man was dressed like the person who helped Yashwant Deshpande. The man approached Gavankar, handed him a parcel saying, "Now I'm going" and left.

Gavankar did not know what was happening for a moment. Then he opened the parcel and was stunned to see that it contained Ram's *murti*. He was overjoyed to see the beautiful idol, but at the same time he was filled with anguish and remorse. He cried out, "*Deva*, I could not recognise you."

## The *bhakari* naivedya is still fresh

He and his family started celebrating *Ram navami* and *Vijay dasami* in their home, in Kurla. He did *annadan* on both these festivals. In 1937,

151

he had a vivid dream. Baba said, *"Bhikshecha bhakari le gode."* (The *bhakari* obtained by *bhiksha* is very sweet.) He got about 50 kgs of *bhajri* (a grain) and *jhunka bhakari* was made out of it. (*Jhunka* is a dry dish made with chopped onions, green chillies and gram flour, it's like a dry *pithla* and *bhakari* is flat bread made from *bhajri* flour and roasted.)

About 200-300 people ate to their hearts content. Before the *annadan* was started, 11 *junka bhakari* was offered to Baba as *naivedya*. Of the *naivedya* offered, one *bhakari* was left in front of Baba's photograph. The rest was made into small pieces and distributed. Wonder of wonders the *bhakari* even after 35 years or more is neither stale, bitter or covered by fungus, nor eaten by ants.

Ref: *Prabhav Shri Sai cha, Dr K B Gavankar thatha Anna Sahib Gavankar yanche jeevan charita*

## Leela 88: The experiences of Krishna Rao Naryana Parulkar

In his letter dated 1-9-1925, he writes that it was a tradition with his father to do *annadan* every year. This was in memory of Shri Dutt Maharaj. Every year he invited a 100 Brahmins to a lavish lunch. If for any reason a year lapsed and the lunch could not be served, the following year 200 Brahmins were invited.

In 1918, when Baba took *mahasamadhi* the *annadan* couldn't be given for some reason. So it was decided to invite 200 Brahmins, and to have the luncheon on one Saturday. The next day which was a Tuesday he got up as usual at 5 a.m. and started doing *naam smaran*. He got an intense desire to invite Kaka Sahib Dixit. A short while later, he was assailed with doubts, "Would Kaka come so far just to have lunch?"

This went on till he did the noon *arati*. He heard Baba clearly say, "Why are you agitated, and getting all these doubts? Write to Kaka, he will come because it's my order. Then make him sit with the

Brahmins and give him a good meal. Know that I will come for the luncheon."

He immediately wrote to Kaka and invited him. He also wrote about his experience. He waited for a reply, and did not receive any confirmation. He felt that if Kaka could not come, it was useless to invite the Brahmins. On Saturday he felt very sad, and his mind was disturbed. Everything was ready, he then went to Baba's photograph and said, "I am a sinner, so you will not come to my home for lunch." Then did *sastang* namaskar and came out.

At that very moment he received a telegram stating that Kaka and Shama were arriving by the 'Delhi Express Train'. His joy knew no bounds. Immediately he and his friends went to the station to receive them.

Then with reverence he made them sit with the Brahmins for the meal, and they had a hearty meal. Parulkar was convinced that Baba had come and had his meal because of Shama's unexpected arrival. He knew that Baba always sent Shama instead of going himself.

Ref: *Sai Leela Margashrish Shake 1847. Ank 9. Year 3 (1925)*

## Leela 89:  Sadashiv Naik's mother attends Bapu's wedding

The wedding of Dixit's son, Bapu, was to be conducted at Khandwa. The dates for the ceremonies were *shasti* 6th and *astmi* the 8th. All the devotees at Harda were invited. At that time Sadashiv Dhundiraj Naik's mother was seriously sick and it seemed she would soon pass away.

There were about 5 days left for the wedding. That evening he (Parulkar) and his friends were discussing the wedding when Krishna Rao Naik said, "I had a keen desire that all of us should attend the wedding, but Sadu's mother is seriously sick and may pass away at any time. It's impossible for him to attend." (Sadashiv, Krishna Rao and Parulkar were friends, and devoted to Baba.)

Early next morning Baba stood before him (Parulkar) and said, "Tell Sadu that his mother will not pass away before the wedding. And all of them should attend the wedding. She will pass away on *ekadashi*." The whole family, including his ailing mother, attended the wedding and had a great time. His mother died on *ekadashi*, just as Baba had predicted.

Ref: *Sai Leela Margashrish Shake 1847. Ank 9. Year 6 (1925)*

## Leela 90: **Baba sends a photograph of his to Sadu Bhayia**

Baba sent His photograph to Sadu Bhayia Naik in 1915, through Balaram and Muktaram. This photograph was kept in Dixit *wada*. On Thursday (*Das Navami*), the 8th of February, it reached his home. Baba sent a message saying, "Through this photograph I have come to your home. Without my permission don't come to Shirdi again."

The photograph was placed on a *sinhasan* (throne). *Puja* and *rudra abhishek* was performed. This was followed by *annadan*. Muktaram climbed up on top of the roof to hoist a flag. It was hoisted three-fourth of the way when his arm ached terribly. Simultaneously Baba seated in the Dwaraka Mai asked a devotee to massage his arm. Baba said, "*Allah Malik. Garrebon ka wali hai. Allah se bada kaun hai?* (Allah *Malik* is the saviour of the poor. Who is greater than Allah?) At that very moment the pain in Muktaram's arm disappeared, and he was able to complete the task.

The flag was hoisted and every one was joyous as Muktaram was safe.

*Leela 91:* # There is an epidemic of plague in Harda

Baba looked after Sadu Bhayia and his family at all times. Once there was an epidemic of plague in Harda, where he lived. Every one fled deserting the village. At the time Sadu Bhayia had gone to his ancestral village called Bhramingaon. It was about 7 miles away, his father was alone at Harda with Baba's photograph. Sadu Bhayia wrote to Baba asking him, what should be done about the plague? He also asked about the photograph, whether it should be left there.

Baba told him to perform *puja* to the photograph daily, and go back to Harda. And his father should be sent to Shirdi was Baba's advice. A few days later two dead rats were found near the photograph. Sadu panicked, so he immediately wrote to Baba again, and consulted him. Baba in his characteristic way said, "Allah *Malik* was there and there was no need to fear." Sadu stayed on in that house and was safe.

## If you don't come and free me in two days my legs will be eaten

Sadu Bhayia had three sons. The eldest was Anand Rao, next was Lakshman Rao, and the youngest was Shankar Rao. Sadu Bhayia took *samadhi* (died) in 1937. The photograph sent by Baba was in Bhramingaon, and it was unattended to. One night Lakshman Rao got a vivid dream, in that dream Baba said, "I came to your home through this photograph and you have discarded me. If you don't come and free me within two days my leg will be eaten away." Lakshman was shocked at this dream, but couldn't understand it. He went to court as usual but he was restless the whole day. He could not do a jot of work.

## Lakshmanrao goes to Bhramingaon

That night he got the same dream. But this time Baba said, "You have not heeded my warning. If you don't come and set me free my leg will be eaten by termites." The dream terrified Lakshman Rao, and the very next day he went to court and applied for leave. Hastily he went to his home in Bhramingaon. When he opened the door he was shocked to see that termites had eaten the wooden frame, and had invaded the photograph, below Baba's big toe.

He took down the photograph and cleaned it. Then he took the photograph to his home in Indore. There he got it recleaned and reframed and kept it in his home. Now Baba in that photograph is being looked after by his daughter Vanitha.

Ref: *As narrated by Sadu Bhayia's descendants*

## Leela 92: Nana Sahib Chandorkar's udi box

Nana Sahib was a blessed person as he was the only devotee who Baba called to Shirdi. Baba sent word to Nana to come, not once but thrice. When he finally came for Baba's *darshan* he asked Baba why he wanted to meet him.

Baba calmly replied, "There are a myriad of human beings on this earth, do I call any of them? So there must be a reason, and that reason is that we have *rinanubandhic* ties for 6 generations."

Gradually his faith increased to such an extent that he became one of the premier apostles of Baba. He was responsible in bringing many influential people, and government officials to Shirdi. Many of the devotees like Dabolkar, and Dixit, were brought by him. Baba on the other hand taught him a philosophy to live life by. This he did through his *leelas*. Then immediately told him where he erred, so he would never forget it. Many of the *leelas* are given above.

Baba also gave him a lot of *udi*; Nana kept some of it in this box and carried the box with him wherever he went. Along with the *udi* Nana kept a small photograph of Baba.

---

*Leela 93:* **Silver padukas**

Das Ganu gave these silver *padukas* to Mina Tai Kuvelekar. She was Nana Sahib Chandorkar's eldest child. She is mentioned in *Shri Sai Satcharita* Chapter 33 'The Jamner Miracle'. Baba sends *udi* to her, so she can deliver safely.

Her husband died of plague in Poona in 1904. Mina Tai was just 17 years old at that time. Mina Tai was pregnant when her husband passed away. She delivered a baby boy in 1905 who died soon after birth. She was devastated by such a great loss; then Das Ganu gave her these *padukas* of Baba. She prayed to them daily and found solace doing so.

---

*Leela 94:* **Silver padukas with chatri**

These silver *padukas* were given to Mrs Oke. She and her family visited Shirdi in 1914. They went to the Dwaraka Mai and Baba gave her these *padukas*. They are with her granddaughter who resides in Poona. She has made a silver *chatri* (umbrella) above the *padukas*.

# Baba's leelas on death and resurrection

Two *leelas* are given below where Baba gives life to a baby goat, while he lets a young boy die. There is always something to be learned from Baba's actions and *leelas*. In the first *leela* Baba resurrects a kid (baby goat).

## A 10-day-old kid (baby goat) dies in the Dwaraka Mai

It was a hot summer day (two days after Holi) in the year 1911, at that time the *sabhamandap* was not constructed. Mrs Tarkhad was seated in the sanctum sanctorum, and talking to Baba. There were a few devotees below, in the *sabhamandap* area. At about 2 o'clock in the afternoon, the *sabhamandap* area was as hot as an oven. A kid (baby goat) about 10 days old walked into the Dwaraka Mai, gasping for breath, it lay down and stopped breathing.

Mrs Tarkhad noticed this and she got up and went to see what had happened. By that time many villagers also went to investigate, if the kid had died. The villagers told her that the kid had died. Extremely saddened by this she went back and told Baba that the baby goat was dead. Baba was sitting near the *katada* (railing) and he saw all this. Baba said, "*Aayi*, it's not dead, but has fainted due to this heat." Mrs Tarkhad kept insisting that the baby goat had died. Then Baba exclaimed, "Really is it dead?" Baba got up, took a tumrel and filled it with water, and went down the steps to where the goat lay. He then tilted the tumrel so that a thin stream of water could flow from it, and did a *pradikahina* (circumbulation) around the dead goat. Thus pouring a circle of water around the goat and also a little water into its mouth.

The goat shivered and started breathing again. The villagers and devotees alike had gathered around Baba to witness the miracle. Turning to Mrs Tarkhad who was standing close by, Baba said, "Aayi look this goat was not dead. As I told you the heat had exhausted it, and it had fainted." The villagers in unison said, "But Baba the goat wasn't breathing." Baba replied, "Now don't crowd around it. The kid will soon jump up, skip and go away." Just as Baba said, the kid jumped up, skipped and ran away. This made every one happy. Turning to Mrs Tarkhad, Baba said, "Look *Aayi,* the kid had fainted from heat exhaustion, and is all right now." Mrs Tarkhad whispered, "Baba the kid was lifeless and not breathing." The villagers went home and Baba and Mrs Tarkhad went into the sanctum sanctorum.

The goat has always been the sacrificial animal from time immemorial. The pundit would hold a *naadi* (sort of nerve) at the throat and say some mantras and the goat would stop breathing. With another set of mantras he could revive it.

The *Shri Sai Satcharita* is replete with *leelas* of goats, e.g. in Chapter 23. Dixit's guru *bhakti* is put to test when an old feeble goat wanders into the Dwaraka Mai. Baba asks him to sacrifice it with one stroke of the knife. Dixit follows Baba's words to the letter, and gets ready to strike the goat. Baba then asks him to stop and the goat finally dies a natural death.

In *Shri Sai Satcharita* Chapter 46, the *leela* of the two brothers who were born as goats is given. The two brothers in their previous life were on amicable terms, but greed and jealousy caused a lot of ill feeling and animosity. As time passed, they became enemies, then one day they killed each other. They were known to Baba, who loved them equally.

In the next reincarnation they became goats, and were passing by when Baba recognised them, and bought them for a large sum. The devotees saw the transaction and were upset. So Baba sends them back to the flock, but after feeding them with lentils.

In the *leela* of the kid that died in the Dwaraka Mai, the *sadguru* i.e., Baba takes the *roopa* of 'Brahma' who is the creator. Here Baba makes a circle of water around the dead kid and gives it life.

Ref: *Sai Leela Ank 5, 6, 7 and 8. Year 7 (1929)*

_Leela 96:_       **Let the boy depart,
don't stand in his way**

The second _leela_ is about a boy who dies and Baba is unwilling to resurrect him. In Shirdi, a lady was devastated as her only child was bitten by a cobra. This happened at about 2 a.m. She ran to the Dwaraka Mai and asked Baba for some _tirth_ to revive her son. Baba did not give the _tirth_, nor did he give her _udi_. She pleaded with him to save her son; finally Baba said, "Don't stand in his path. Let the boy depart."

The mother was disappointed; she left after some time. The next morning the boy died. Kaka Dixit came to know about this and he fell at Baba's feet begging him to resurrect the boy.

Finally Baba said, "Bhau, don't get involved in this turmoil. This child's lifespan is over for this body. He will take up a new body. In that new body he will perform some good deeds. But if I resurrect him, because of your request, he will come back to this very same body, and will lead a mundane life. If his life is given back, the good deeds that he was to perform in his reincarnation will come to naught. The third reincarnation will be that of a goat. So it's not as simple as it looks on the surface. Of course, as a goat he will not be able to perform any good deeds. Are you willing to take responsibility for this? So Bhau, do not plead for the resurrection of this boy."

With this explanation Dixit was satisfied and pleaded no further. He also got a good lesson on rebirth. In this _leela_ the _sadguru_ (Baba) takes the _roopa_ or form of _Rudra_ (destroyer) and does not give _udi tirth_ to the mother and does not revive her son.

Ref: _Sai Leela Ank 5, 6, 7 and 8. Year 7_

## The boy from Nadia is given four more years to live

In conclusion, on the subject of death and dying, the author 'Mahatara' (Baba called Baba Sahib Tarkhad by this name) gives another *leela* where four years were added to a boy's life.

In the town of Nadia, a famous astrologer predicted that the sub judge's son would die at the age of 17. The grandmother of this lad had intense faith in the saint, Shri Bhaskar Anand Saraswati. She prayed to him to save the lad. The saint responded and said the child would live as long as he did. And so it came to pass.

Four years later, the saint contracted cholera when he was at Kashi and died two days later. The lad in Nadia fell off a horse and succumbed to head injury at the very moment that the saint passed away. Thus defying astrology and even the normal course of life.

In conclusion, to an ordinary devotee like me it's confusing; on one hand Baba saves the life of a goat, while he lets the boy die. Baba, however, knew the past, present and future. That boy was destined to achieve some good karma in his next life, which he couldn't in the present body. As for the goat, possibly the *rinanubandhic* ties between it and Baba were strong.

The author says that the grandmother of the lad at Nadia had such intense faith that death was forced to go away. Faith, when it's very intense, and comes from the heart and soul, can help a devotee face any difficult hurdle of life. It can defy astrology and even the normal course of life itself.

In this *leela*, the *sadguru* (Bhaskar Anand Saraswati) takes the *roopa* of Vishnu, who is the preserver. Here he preserves the child's life for four more years. Ref: *Sai Leela Ank 4, 5, 6, 7 and 8. Year 7*

## Leela 97: Shri Bapu Vaidya offers unripe green Alfanso mangoes to Baba

Around 1917 or so, Jog resided in Kavad. His house was next to the Kavad *Sansthan*. From Bhivandi, a friend named Vaidya, came to Kavad and visited Jog. A few days later, Jog wanted to visit Shirdi and Vaidya accompanied him.

Just before they left, his friend went to the orchard in front of the house and plucked some Alfanso mangoes. The mangoes, though large, were quite raw. Jog wasn't too happy with this. Another devotee named Lakshman Shastri Lele, who was in charge of the orchard, was quite annoyed with what Vaidya had done. Lele said, "Though the mangoes are huge they are quite green and unripe. At least if they were ripe and you had plucked them, it would have been all right. Now what are you going to do with these unripe mangoes?"

Vaidya told him that he wanted to offer them to Baba. Lele, still annoyed said, "If they were ripe I would have given them to you myself." Vaidya told him that they were going to Shirdi right away hence, he had plucked them.

Jog did not like the idea of offering raw mangoes to Baba, so he bought some ripe Alfanso mangoes. They reached the Dwaraka Mai and Jog offered the ripe mangoes, while Vaidya kept the unripe mangoes in the room. Baba, however, pushed the ripe mangoes to one side and said, "Give me the mangoes you brought from Kavad." Jog told him that they were very green and raw. Baba insisted that Jog should give him those raw mangoes, so he went and fetched them and placed them before Baba.

Baba held the mangoes by their stem and raised his hand so that they were at eye level. With concentration and intensity he looked at them for a while. At that time, tears of joy rolled down his cheeks, for he perceived the love in Vaidya's offering. Then he asked Jog to cut and distribute them to the devotees seated there. Baba then asked them what the mangoes tasted like. In unison they answered, "Extremely sweet and delectable." Turning to Jog, who had eaten a piece, he said, "Bapu Sahib didn't you say that these mangoes were green and raw?"

Vaidya was wonderstruck and his faith in Baba became firm and intense. When Jog went to Kavad, he told Lele and everyone about this *leela*. After this *leela*, Jog never ever forgot to bring Alfanso mangoes for Baba. Every time he went to Kavad, Jog brought the mangoes whether they were ripe or unripe.

Ref: *Sai Leela Ank 5, 6, 7 and 8. Year 7 (1929)*

## Leela 98: Baba sends Balaram to Machindragad

Balaram was a devotee from Bandra. He was affluent and had a business enterprise. The death of his wife devastated him. His mind was restless and he had no interest in his business. He handed over his business to his son, and decided to seek refuge at Shirdi. It was his good karmas of past life that brought him to Shirdi. Mankar then made Shirdi his home.

In Shirdi he spent his time doing Baba's *seva*. But even these spiritual surroundings would not calm his mind. The compassionate Baba said, "Your days at Shirdi are over. Take these 12 rupees for the journey ahead. Go to Machindragad and do *tapasya* (penance) and meditation there."

It is appropriate here to disclose the meaning of the 12 rupees.

It's the *tapasya* or penance of the twelve inner disciplines, they are as follows: 1. *Viveka* (discrimination), 2. *Vairagya* (renunciation), 3. *Nishwartha* (selflessness), 4. *Sama* (calmness), 5. *Dama* (self-control),

163

6. *Uparati* (self-withdrawal), 7. *Titiksha* (forbearance), 8. *Samadhan* (self-settled), 9. *Shradha* (faith), 10. *Satsang* (holy company), 11. *Maun* (silence of the mind), 12. *Ekanta Dhyan* (solitude and meditation) and last but not the least, 'Guru's grace', for without it nothing is possible.

Balaram was reluctant to go at first, but then he thought it was not wise to object his guru's advice. So he left for Machindragad. It was calm and peaceful, and he meditated there.

One morning just as he finished mediating Baba gave him *shakshatkar*. Mankar asked Baba why he was sent here. Baba replied, "शिर्डी सोडून बाहेर कुठेही तुझ्या दृष्टीने मी नव्हतो. आता बघून घे. तेव्हा तो मी तिथे होतो, तोच मी आता इथे आहे।।"

"Outside of Shirdi you thought I did not exist. Now see for yourself. The same Baba is here as he was at Shirdi." Baba showed Balaram his omnipresence.

This *gad* is in Sangli *zilla*, and the *talluqa* of Islampur. On the *gad* there is the *samadhi* of Machindranath. There is a temple of Gowrakshanath which is atop the *gad*, there are about 800 steps to reach there. It takes about an hour to reach and there are no facilities to stay there. Every year in the month of April the *punyatithi* of Machindranath is celebrated there with great pomp and show.

Ref: *Sai Anantha Varsh 2. July 2007*

# Conclusion

This book contains information, *leelas* and sayings of the *sadguru* (Baba) gathered from various sources. These stories, the pranks that he played, give the human side of the *sadguru*. Any devotee, when faced with a difficult situation, usually turns to God, a teacher, mentor or a friend. And Baba is all of these, so it is rather easy to confide in him. He is that friend who stands by you through thick and thin.

His *vaani* (sayings) and teachings can be used by any devotee in their daily lives. It will help in the devotee's spiritual growth and upliftment.

■■■

NEW

The Miracles of Sai Baba
ISBN 978 81 207 5433 1 (HB)
₹ 250

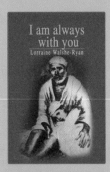

I am always with you
*Lorraine Walshe-Ryan*
ISBN 978 81 207 3192 9
₹ 150

Unravelling the Enigma: Shirdi
Sai Baba in the light of Sufism
*Marianne Warren*
ISBN 978 81 207 2147 0
₹ 400

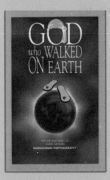

God Who Walked on Earth:
The Life & Times of
Shirdi Sai Baba
*Rangaswami Parthasarathy*
ISBN 978 81 207 1809 8
₹ 150

The Thousand Names of
Shirdi Sai Baba
Sri B.V. Narasimha Swami Ji
Hindi translation by
*Dr. Rabinder Nath Kakarya*
ISBN 978 81 207 3738 9
₹ 75

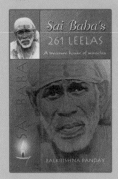

Sai Baba's 261 Leelas
*Balkrishna Panday*
ISBN 978 81 207 2727 4
₹ 125

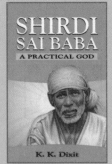

Shirdi Sai Baba
A Practical God
*K. K. Dixit*
ISBN 978 81 207 5918 3
₹ 75

Spotlight on the Sai Story
*Chakor Ajgaonker*
ISBN 978 81 207 4399 1
₹ 125

Shri Sai Baba- The Saviour
*Dr. Rabinder Nath Kakarya*
ISBN-978-81-207-4701-2
₹ 100

Life History of Shirdi Sai Baba
*Ammula Sambasiva Rao*
ISBN 978 81 207 2033 4
₹ 150

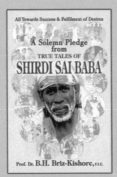

A Solemn Pledgefrom
True Tales of Shirdi Sai Baba
*Dr B H Briz-Kishore*
ISBN 978 81 207 2240 8
₹ 95

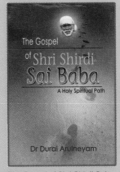

The Gospel of Shri Shirdi Sai
Baba:
A Holy Spiritual Path
*Dr Durai Arulneyam*
ISBN 978 81 207 3997 0
₹ 150

Shri Shirdi Sai Baba: His
Life and Miracles
ISBN 978 81 207 2877 6
₹ 25

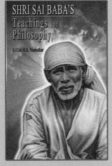

Shri Sai Baba's Teachings &
Philosophy
*Lt Col M B Nimbalkar*
ISBN 978 81 207 2364 1
₹ 90

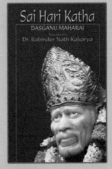

Sai Hari Katha
Dasganu Maharaj Translated by
*Dr. Rabinder Nath Kakarya*
ISBN 978 81 207 3324 4
₹ 100

Sai Baba: His Divine Glimpses
*V B Kher*
ISBN 978 81 207 2291 0
₹ 95

Sri Sai Baba
Swami Sai Sharan Anand
*Translated by V.B Kher*
ISBN 978 81 207 1950 7
₹ 200

Shirdi Sai Baba and
other Perfect Masters
*C B Satpathy*
ISBN 978 2384 15081 207 9
₹ 150

Baba's Rinanubandh
Leelas during His Sojoum in Shirdi
*Compiled by Vinny Chitluri*
ISBN 978 81 207 3403 6
₹ 200

Baba's Vaani: His Sayings and
Teachings
*Compiled by Vinny Chitluri*
ISBN 978 81 207 3589 1
₹ 200

Baba's Gurukul
SHIRDI
*Vinny Chitluri*
ISBN-978-81-207-4770-8
₹ 200

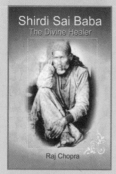

Shirdi Sai Baba
The Divine Healer
*Raj Chopra*
ISBN 978 81 207 4766 1
₹ 100

Baba's Vaani: His Sayings and
Teachings
Compiled by Vinny Chitluri
ISBN 978 81 207 3589 1
₹ 200

Guru Charitra
Shree Swami Samarth
ISBN 978 81 207 3348 0
₹ 200

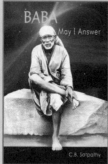

BABA- May I Answer
*C.B. Satpathy*
ISBN 978 81 207 4594 0
₹ 150

Sri Narasimha Swami
Apostle of Shirdi Sai Baba
Dr. G.R. Vijayakumar
ISBN 978 81 207 4432 5
₹ 90

Lord Sri Dattatreya
The Trinity
Dwarika Mohan Mishra
ISBN 978 81 207 5417 1
₹ 200

108 Names of Shirdi Sai Baba
ISBN 978 81 207 3074 8
₹ 50

Shirdi Sai Speaks...
Sab Ka Malik Ek
Quotes for the Day
ISBN 81 207 3101   200978 1
₹ 200

Shirdi Sai Speaks...
Sab Ka Malik Ek
Quotes for the Day
ISBN 81 207 3101   200978 1
₹ 200

बाबा का ऋणानुबंध
शिरडी में उनके तहवास के दौरान रची लीलाएँ
संकलनः विनी चितलुरी
अनुवादकः बेला शर्मा
ISBN 978 81 207 5998 5
₹ 125

श्री साई सच्चरित्रा
डॉ रबिन्द्र नाथ ककरिया
ISBN 978 81 207 2501 0  ₹ 250 (PB)
ISBN 978 81 207 2500 3  ₹ 300 (PB)

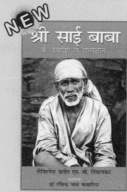

श्री साई बाबा
के उपदेश व तत्त्वज्ञान
लेफ्टिनेन्ट कर्नल एम. बी. निंबालकर
अनुवादकः डॉ रबिन्द्र नाथ ककरिया
ISBN 978 81 207 5971 8
₹ 100

साई बाबा एक अवतार
बेला शर्मा
ISBN 978 81 207 5971 8
₹ 100

बाबा का अनुराग
समर्पित भक्तों के प्रति स्नेह–प्यार
संकलनः विनी चितलुरी
अनुवादकः डॉ. रबिन्द्र नाथ ककरिया
ISBN 978 81 207 6699 0
₹ 100

बाबा का गुरुकुलः शिरडी
संकलनः विनी चितलुरी
अनुवादकः डॉ. रबिन्द्र नाथ ककरिया

ISBN 978 81 207 6698 3
₹ 125

श्री साई बाबा के परम भक्त
डॉ रबिन्द नाथ ककरिया
ISBN 978 81 207 2779 3
₹ 75

साई हरि कथा
दसगणु महाराज
ISBN 978 81 207 3323 7
₹ 65

साई हरि कथा
दसगणु महाराज
ISBN 978 81 207 3323 7
₹ 65

साई दत्तावधूता
राजेन्द्र भण्डारी
ISBN 978 81 207 4400 4
₹ 125

श्री शीरडी साई बाबा व अन्य सदगुरू
चन्द्रभानु सतपथी
ISBN 978 81 207 44011
₹ 90

बाबा आध्यात्मिक विचार
चन्द्रभानु सतपथी
ISBN 978 81 207 4627 5
₹ 100

बाबा की वाणी उनके वचन तथा उपदेश
बेला शर्मा
ISBN 978-81-207-4745-6
₹ 100

श्रीनरसिम्हा स्वामी
शिरडी साई बाबा के दिव्य प्रचारक
डॉ रबिन्द नाथ ककरिया
ISBN 978-81-207-4437 0
₹ 75

शिरडी साई बाबा
प्रो डॉ बी एच ब्रिज-किशोर
ISBN 978 81 207 2346 7
₹ 60

साई भक्तानुभव
डॉ. रबिन्द्र नाथ ककरिया
ISBN 978 81 207 3052 6
₹ 90

श्री साई बाबा के अनन्य भक्त
डॉ. रबिन्द्र नाथ ककरिया
ISBN 978 81 207 2705 5
₹ 85

साई का संदेश
डॉ. रबिन्द्र नाथ ककरिया
ISBN 978 81 207 2879 0
₹ 125

शिरडी संपूर्ण दर्शन
डॉ रबिन्द्र नाथ ककरिया
ISBN 978 81 207 2312 2
₹ 50

मुक्तिदाता श्री साई बाबा
डॉ रबिन्द्र नाथ ककरिया
ISBN 978 81 207 2778 6
₹ 65

शिरडी सांई बाबा
विकास कपूर
ISBN 978 81 207 5969 5
₹ 30

साई शरण में
चन्द्रभानु सतपथी
ISBN 978 81 207 2802 8
₹ 150

पृथ्वी पर अवतरित भगवान
शिरडी के साई बाबा
रंगास्वामी पार्थसारथी
ISBN 978 81 207 2802 8
₹ 150

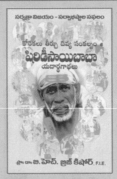

For detailed Catalogue visit our website
www.sterlingpublishers.com
E-mail:mail@sterlingpublishers.com